MW00795536

SADDLE SAVVY

A Guide to the Western Saddle

Other publications by Dusty Johnson

BOOK

1993, *Saddlemaking - Lessons in Construction, Repair and Evaluation*

VIDEO

1993, *Saddlemaking - Lessons in Construction, Repair and Evaluation* (115 min.)

1995, *Chaps - Lessons in Construction of Western and Motorcycle Style Chaps* (35 min.)

1996, *Holsters - Lessons in Construction of Holsters and Knife Sheaths* (65 min.)

SADDLE
SAVVY

A Guide to the Western Saddle

by
Dusty Johnson
Pleasant Valley Saddle Shop

Illustrated by Doug Zender

SADDLEMANPRESS™
Loveland, Colorado

Cover carving: Bob Dellis
Illustrations: Doug Zender
Photographs: Dusty Johnson
Editorial Assistance: Sharon Johnson

First Edition: January 1999

Publisher's Cataloging-in-Publication Data
Johnson, Dusty
    Saddle Savvy : a guide to the western saddle / by
Dusty Johnson ; illustrated by Doug Zender. -- 1st ed.

    p.cm.
    Includes bibliographical references and index
    LCCCN 98-96853
    ISBN 0-9639164-4-0

    1. Western saddles. I. Zender, Doug. II. Title

TS1032.J65 19999   685'.1
                                      QBI98-1583

Dedication

*This book is dedicated to
all saddlemakers, past and present,
sung and unsung,
who have
devoted their time and talent
to improving western saddles
for
man and beast alike*

and to

my very patient and loving wife
Sharon
*who has put up with this cowboy
and his leather "stuff"
for
many, many years*

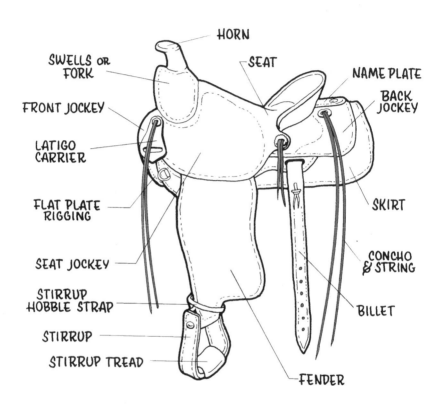

HORN

SWELLS OR FORK

SEAT

NAME PLATE

FRONT JOCKEY

BACK JOCKEY

LATIGO CARRIER

FLAT PLATE RIGGING

SKIRT

SEAT JOCKEY

CONCHO & STRING

STIRRUP HOBBLE STRAP

BILLET

STIRRUP

STIRRUP TREAD

FENDER

Table of Contents

FOREWORD

From the first page, as the reader of this volume, you will recognize that the author is a knowledgeable and thoroughly trained leatherworker. Dusty has the necessary skills and background to accurately and concisely convey information on saddlery, not only for the professional horseman and cowboy, but more importantly for the recreational rider. All readers will gain new and profitable insights into the process of building and buying their next saddle through the guidance of this book.

I have known Dusty Johnson for ten years and have found in him a most enthusiastic teacher of leatherwork in his Pleasant Valley Saddlemaking School. He is a most informative and talented writer of saddle methodology, and a willing individual in sharing his knowledge of leatherwork, saddlery and other aspects of western culture and arts as well.

The real beauty of *Saddle Savvy* lies in the simple fact that this book and the saddle making principles it will share shall remain timeless. You'll find it a reliable, convenient reference and guidebook for years to come. Its size and Western flair may make it a companion in your saddlebag for many chats around the campfire.

Bill Reis, Publisher
The Leather Crafters & Saddlers Journal

PREFACE

I have been around horsemen and craftsmen from my childhood. I've also been employed with working ranches and livery stables. To me tack choices seemed to come naturally after spending so many hours in the saddle with the "top hands". It wasn't until I became a saddlemaker and observed a wide variety of horsemen that I realized they were struggling with decisions about their single most expensive horse related item ... the saddle.

I had never thought of selecting a saddle as a difficult or confusing process. As I watched my new friends and associates bounce from one choice to another in saddle styles and types I realized how confusing it must be for someone new to horse activities to make an educated decision about selecting a saddle.

I decided it was time to make the saddle selection process easier by writing this book. I will discuss each part of the saddle in detail, explaining it's use and function. I will offer enough information and opinion about each part to help you make decisions based on more than tradition, fable and guesswork. I hope to remove the stress from what should be a great experience.

Things western should be relaxed and stress free like the western lifestyle itself. When you walk into a saddle shop you should be able to enjoy the unmistakable aroma of tanned leather. You should be able to admire the beauty and functionality of a fine saddle. Your visit to a saddle shop should be fun and exciting. Don't be confused by a well intentioned friend's "expert" opinion. Remember, if you have five horsemen in a room, you'll probably have six opinions on any one subject.

Don't make a choice based on tradition. Traditions can be misleading ... as a newlywed, my wife served a beautiful ham at a family gathering. It was colorful and the ends were trimmed neatly. When the meal was over, I asked her why she cut the ends off the ham. Without hesitatiion she told me her mother did it that way. Curious about this odd family tradition, I asked my mother-in-law where she learned to trim the ham in that fashion. She credited her mother. Since Grandma was present at this feast I questioned her, "Grandma, why do you trim the ends off the ham?" She thought a minute and answered, "My pan was too small." So much for tradition!

Unless everything in a man's memory of childhood is

misleading, there is a time when an impression lasting only a few seconds may be imprinted for life. There are occasions, when I step into a tackroom or onto a backporch cluttered with old saddles and gear, that I am instantly transported back to being a boy of eight or ten years old. Deeply breathing the aroma of saddle blankets, leather conditioning oils and well used saddles brings on a sense of peacefulness and excitement together. It floods me with memories of quiet rides in summer pastures, warm barns in winter, gentle and trustworthy ponies and of horses too marvelous to ever forget completely. The fun and excitement I felt when first becoming familiar with horses and the equipment used with them is a joy that should be experienced by everyone.

Leather is universal in its appeal. The first statement usually made by anyone stepping into my saddle shop is "Wow! It sure smells good in here!" Fresh leather demands attention. It needs to be touched and admired!The appeal of leather is even more compelling when it is crafted into fine objects; wallets, belts, handbags, clothing, furniture, etc. The ultimate leather object, the item that arouses the most imagery in most people's minds, is a saddle ... a western saddle!

Depending on background and viewpoint, a saddle brings to mind pioneering times, rodeos, trail rides, Casey Tibbs, Jim Shoulders, Larry Mahan, Henry Fonda, Jimmy Stewart, John Wayne, The Lone Ranger, Gene Autry and Roy Rogers. It can remind us of hard days working on a ranch, trail rides in beautiful countryside, an exciting rodeo or a leisurely ride at a livery stable near a vacation resort.

It is this excitement with saddles and all things associated with them that led me to becoming a saddlemaker. Being a craftsman in leather keeps me close to that nostalgic aroma and enables me to share some of that mystery and joy with my customers and saddlemaking students.

When an author first decides to write a book the questions that must be answered are; "Does anyone need this information? Is this book necessary? Will this book make the reader's life easier or save them money?" It didn't take too much examination to answer these questions with a resounding "Yes!".

After careful observation, I can honestly say that most horsemen don't really know beans about the saddle they use every day. Ranchers and working cowboys usually have an excellent "feel" for what makes a good saddle, but they cannot readily point out why a particular outfit is made a certain way or why they prefer one style over another. I often hear "Well, it's just the right way. The way it has always been done." Many times there is a better way and tradition has interferred with logic and well informed decisions.

Newcomers to the horse world are faced with many conflicting opinions about saddles and their functions. They can be overwhelmed with the choices of style, construction and materials. Even the names of the parts seem foreign, at first, and lead to confusion and misunderstanding.

A saddle should not be considered a disposable item. It is costly enough that it must be considered a long-term investment. Great care must be given to its selection. More than beauty alone must be judged. Comfort, quality and durability have to be factored into the decision.

I want this book to be your guide through the experience of choosing the right saddle. Read it first and then visit your saddlemaker. Talk to him about his work, materials, style and opinions. Refer back to *Saddle Savvy* until you are comfortable with your choices. Keep in mind, you don't need to purchase a saddle for each purpose or for every horse. You want one saddle that can be used for work or pleasure; a saddle that will always be enjoyable to own and ride. A good rig is a joy to ride. And, as the years go by, it will continue to provide just as much pleasure to look at and admire for its quality, endurance and the memories it will contain. Whether you are purchasing a new saddle or shopping for a used rig, I hope this book will make the decisions easier.

Happy Trails and Good Riding, my friends,
Dusty Johnson

SADDLE LEATHER

The two major components of a good saddle are the **tree** and the **leather**. As any real horse person knows the very best saddles are made of natural leather. Why do we find leather is always the best? Why do people *in the know* always insist upon genuine leather? Prestige, durability, eye appeal, and unsurpassed beauty are some of the many qualities inherent in this product of nature.

From the earliest civilizations right up to the present time, leather has been held in high esteem by people throughout the world. Supporting this fact are the large number of leather articles which archeologists have unearthed and a frequent mention of the tanner in the pages of recorded history. Man's high regard for leather is due in no small part to a unique combination of desirable physical properties, incredible variability, and just plain good looks. But there are reasons beyond this—things which only nature can build into a substance.

Nature's products affect our senses and our emotions. Psychologists call this property the *aesthetic appeal* of a substance. Though it varies in intensity from person to person an aesthetic sense is present in all of us. The universal appreciation of nature's products is an established fact. Man-made or synthetic products, on the other hand, usually fail to arouse our aesthetic senses.

Leather is an extraordinary example of a product that has enjoyed universal appeal throughout the ages. Just the sound of the word leather arouses the senses and conjurs up the image of fine quality. Anyone who has ever held a fine leather holster or a top quality leather jacket has experienced the sensation of holding something with richness.

The process of making leather is unrivaled for pure craftsmanship and chemical ingenuity. The practice of preserving skins pre-dates recorded history. For this reason, we don't know very much about the methods used by primitive men. It is evident, however, that as time went on, tanning grew into a highly developed art. The Egyptians carved pictures into stone more than five thousand years ago depicting planners at work. By the year 500 B.C. the Greeks had developed leathermaking into a very well established trade. We also know that, by this time, mankind had discovered that various leaves and barks of certain trees, when soaked in water, would produce solutions with a capacity to tan leather.

In the 12th century, tanner's guilds were organized in England to help supervise the manufacturing processes and, by adhering to strict standards, they advanced the art of leathermaking. In America the early settlers found that tanning was well-known to the Indians and they were quick to adapt their methods in producing buckskin for their clothing needs. Their process was basically handed down from generation to generation. Modern tanning methods have changed considerably. The two most important developments in tanning were the thermometer and the hydrometer.

By using the *thermometer*, the tanner could determine the temperature of his solutions more accurately than the human finger was capable of doing. The *hydrometer* told him the density, or strength, of his solutions — with far greater precision than his sense of taste. Recently the development of the *electronic pH meter,* which is used to determine the acidity, or alkalinity of a solution, has given the tanner another tool in controlling the rate various chemical reactions take place. Today, the electron microscope, spectrophotometer, and data processor have been added to the tools of the tanner's trade.

Tanning is one of the world's most respected sciences — a process that today has grown into a highly developed technology. The tanner is proud of his products and is proud to be associated with the goods that are made from them. He stands ready and anxious to produce new leathers to meet the demands of the future.

There is no end to the variety of leathers that are commercially available today. For the purpose of this book, however, we're only interested in the leathers that will be used in the saddle. Those leathers commonly are produced from the hides of cattle. These hides are obtained from the many beef processing plants throughout the world. Hides and skins are by-products of the beef industry. The beef industry in the United States is one of the largest sources of cattle and steerhides for tanning in the world. Every year U.S. tanneries convert many millions of raw hides and skins into leather.

Just as meat is perishable, so too are hides and skins. If not cleaned and treated to prevent putrefication, they begin to decompose and lose leather making substances within hours after removal from the carcass. The protective treatment administered to the hide is termed *curing*. The processing of hides and skins into leather is a fascinating procedure that requires many steps. It includes with soaking, de-hairing, trimming, fleshing, pickling, and finally the tanning.

The actual chemistry involved in tanning is quite complex and well beyond the scope of this book. As with so many other things in this world, man first discovered certain practical methods of achieving something that satisfied his needs without actually knowing many of whys and wherefores. All that is really necessary to know, with regarding the leather in the saddle, are the two basic tanning methods commonly referred to as *chrome tanned* and *vegetable tanned.*

Chrome-tanned indicates a leather which has been prepared with soluble chromium salts, primarily basic chromium sulfate. Currently, this is the most widely used tannage in the USA. However, it is not the leather which you generally want in a fine quality saddle. On the other hand, vegetable tanned (or *bark tanned*) is your best material for a top grade saddle. There are other methods of tanning: retan, oil tanned and latigo leathers which are used in parts of the saddle. I will discuss these leathers while speaking about the parts for which they will be used.

Leather is a natural material made from the hides of animals. Just as no two animals are exactly alike, no two pieces of leather will be identical. In addition to its own genetic heritage, each hide bears little knicks and scars that marked the animal during its lifetime. These natural characteristics are not defects and are considered "marks of distinction" or *the natural beauty of the leather*, adding to the unique appeal of the individual who chose the hide and the finished product.

It takes the equivalent of a complete cowhide to build a saddle. *Saddle skirting* (the name given to heavy hides used in saddle making) is shipped from tanneries as "sides". A side is half of a full hide which has been divided along the backbone. The quality of saddle skirting can vary tremendously among tanneries and the saddle maker has the choice of ordering different weights (thickness) as well as grades (quality) of skirting. Even the best skirting from the top tanneries will show some irregularities of texture, surface blemishes and cuts created during the skinning process. An experienced saddlemaker will evaluate a side of leather and cut the saddle parts according to the required firmness and thickness, all the while avoiding irregularities that would be a blemish on the saddle.

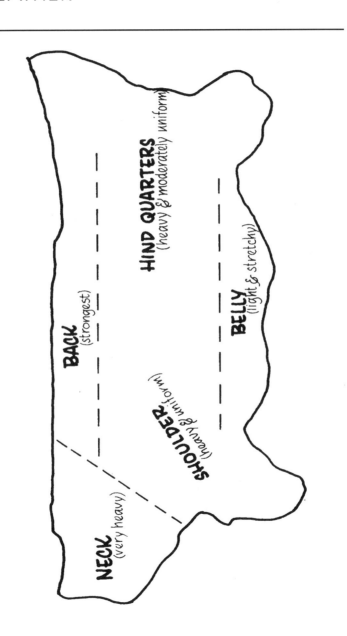

Leather is an interesting material ... sometimes fibrous with a lot of stretch and other times very firm and dense. Firm leather is characterized by close spacing of hair follicles on the grain (smooth) side. Firm leather has closer packing of leather fibers than does softer "flanky" leather which may have a lot of stretchability. Flanky leather is generally used only when a lot of stretch is required, such as on the fork and the cantle binding. These items are primarily cosmetic and don't require great stability or strength in the leather for safety's sake.

Each part of the saddle requires a specific firmness and thickness. For example, stirrup leathers, fenders, billets, rear cinches and the seat are cut from the firm heavy leather that covers the hind quarters and the backbone. These areas are characterized by dense fibers on the flesh (rough) side and have very little stretch. Lighter weight leather from the belly and around the legs of the hide is used for the fork, cantle back, and stirrup covers because it can be stretched around the irregular shapes. As mentioned, much of this leather is a bit flanky and lacks strength and firmness. It has considerable stretch and the fibers on the flesh side are not closely packed.

When evaluating leather used in making the saddle, look at the grain and flesh sides. The grain side may show range scratches but it should be free of major scars such as brands and deep scars that have healed. Many of the light (or fine line) scars, which are not significant to the duty or the utility of the leather, will show as dark streaks when freshly oiled. This is because the scar tissue absorbs more oil than the surrounding flesh. This is only natural and to be expected, however, after a few hours, the fresh oil will spread evenly throughout and this type of minor blemish will no longer show.

When examining the leather in a saddle flex it where possible. The grain surface should not crack, nor should it ooze out excess oils. The flesh side should be free of cuts and the fibers should feel quite dense in the areas were strength this required, such as the stirrup leathers. Check the full length of the stirrup leathers and any leather used in the rigging to be sure it is firm, uniform in thickness and shows the ability to withstand stress.

To retain its purity and other desirable qualities, leather requires conditioning to replace the natural lubricants lost during normal use. Unless provided with proper care and protection, excessive dryness can cause leather to crack and too much moisture may cause it to swell up, mildew, and eventually stiffen as it dries out. Remember, once leather has been damaged the hide can never repair itself. You can help it with oils and preparations to stop any further degeneration, but it can never *grow* a new surface on the skin.

Unprotected leather is highly susceptible to spotting from water and other liquids. A newly purchased saddle should be treated immediately to help prevent permanent stains from occurring. A custom saddlemaker will do this for you prior to delivery. Many low priced manufactured saddles look good, but are coated with a lacquer finish. This is the wrong coating to use as it will prevent further oiling and will probably crack and peel when flexed.

The use of too much oil or wax, however, can clog the pores in the leather. When this happens, leather loses its ability to allow air in and moisture out. Even worse, oils and waxes attract dirt and dust particles which actually cut and tear the microscopic fibers that make leathers of strong and durable.

In a later chapter of this book I will discuss leather care in much more detail. The biggest mistake generally seen is over-oiling, causing the leather to feel mushy and lose much of its strength. With proper care the saddle made of quality leather should last for two or three generations.

Leather Carving courtesy Bob Dellis

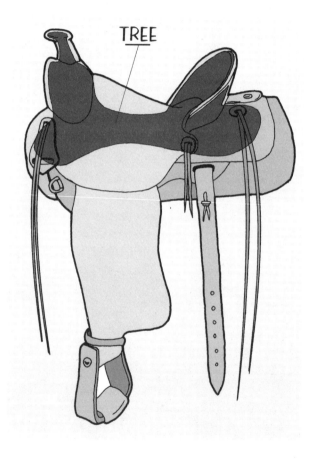

TREE

TREES
(and saddle fitting)

This is probably the first chapter many people will turn to. Today we hear and read a great deal about "Saddle fitting". Everyone tells us how to fit a saddle to a horse. We read in all the horse magazines that a horse can't perform properly unless the saddle fits him perfectly. Horror stories are told about the terrible saddle sores that some horses suffer due to poor fitting saddles. And most importantly, we hear from our friends [who tell us they are "experts" in all things equine] that they know of *someone* who knows *someone* who knows a custom saddlemaker with a measuring device that insures a perfect fit for your horse. As a result of all of this information about saddle fitting, it becomes very difficult to go out and purchase a saddle without feeling as though we've wasted our money and our time and, perhaps, obtained a leather-covered device that will ruin our horse's health and usefulness forever!

Allow me to make a big statement. A statement that is
a little dramatic, yet should put your mind at ease.
***There is no such thing as fitting a saddle to a horse!
It can't be done!*** There, I've said it, don't you feel
better?

Now before you slam the cover shut and go off
muttering bad things about this book and me, allow
me to explain, in detail, why I have made such a strong
statement. I truly believe that saddle fitting is one of
the "urban myths" that has taken on a life of its own.
It's one of those things that sounds good and feels good
to talk about. After all, doesn't this show that we're
concerned about Old Dobbin's welfare? But who have
you ever talked to who can truly show you how to
evaluate the saddle's fit on your horse?

How *can* you fit a saddle to a horses back? Take into
consideration that a horse's conformation changes as
he ages. A saddle that perfectly fits a 3 year-old will
not fit as well when that same horse is 7, 12, or 16. A
horse's shape can also change considerably from season
to season. Horses who wintered well will be fat and
soft in the spring. Those same horses might be lean
and hard by the end of fall. Horses get a little bit more
sway in their backs with age and a little wider with
feed. What happens to their conformation after an
extended period of illness? All of these things will

change the way a saddle fits. At what point do we make the saddle fit perfectly?

How about the working cowboy? He sometimes changes ranches and each ranch will provide him with a string of horses. How long do you suspect he could keep his job if his saddle makes the boss's horses sore? How may saddles can a working cowboy afford? What about the professional horse trainer? A professional trainer usually owns three or four good saddles. This makes good sense as he can choose the best fitting saddle for each horse. However, are any of these saddles "perfect fit"? And consider the hobby horseman who is fortunate enough to have a number of horses. How many saddles does he own? Are they made for each horse he owns?

If the saddle could be made to fit a horse perfectly for his entire life, shouldn't that saddle be sold with the horse when you find a new steed? What should we do with the saddle, the one that fits one horse so perfectly, when the horse dies? Take the saddle out behind the barn and shoot it!?

Don't get me wrong, there is such a thing as a bad fitting saddle, but we're not fitting a fine pair of Italian shoes here. I feel that people have obsessed for too long over the fit of the saddle. Make it simple for

What should we do with the saddle
... shoot it?

yourself and stick with something that looks good and works well on the type of horses that you generally ride.

Before you can begin to evaluate how a saddle sits on the horse's back look carefully at that back to determine its ability to accept a saddle. There are several things to consider. First, the withers should be of sufficient height. Ideally the withers should be level with or a little above the highest point of the croup, or rump, when the horse is standing flat on level ground. Excessively high withers are prone to pressure from saddle trees with low or wide gullets. This would cause soreness because of the pressures in this area. A well muscled back is also important, and smooth muscling is the ideal.

Look at the length of the animal's back. The classic short top line and long bottom line is best. The overly short back can be a problem with the saddle digging into the horse, but the back that is too long is much more common. A horse with a long back often has weak loins, prominent hips, shallow wither muscling, and sometimes steep shoulders. Shoulders that are too prominent are another real concern. With each step the horse takes he pushes the shoulders into the tree bars.

The horse that is narrow through shoulders can also be

a problem. The saddle tends to ride forward onto the shoulder blades, especially when the horse is ridden downhill. He should not be heavily muscled, yet adequate muscling is very important. His legs should be set nicely under the shoulders, with not too steep a shoulder angle. Also very desirable is a good depth to the girth, giving an oval body shape which is very comfortable to ride and should hold a saddle very well. A horse with a round body type and heavy muscling usually has almost no withers. This kind of horse doesn't have a back that will hold anything in place. It would be hard for any saddlemaker to build a saddle that would stay in place.

Another problematic confirmation is the "downhill" back, in which the withers are lower than the croup or point of the hip. With this kind of conformation the saddletree would push against the shoulder blades and make the horse sore in a short time. This would be especially true if the horse were used for cutting or roping.

The ideal conformation, when evaluating what would be good for a saddle, is a well-proportioned body, combining depth of girth, a short back, and a long underline. The back should have smooth muscling over the shoulders, withers, and ribcage, with good strength out into the loin area. The withers should be of good height and moderately long, providing a stable place for the saddle to sit. Long shoulders would allow the cinch to sit well behind the front legs and smooth muscling will allow the shoulders to move freely under the saddletree. This type of confirmation will allow the horse's back to carry a saddle very well with least amount of cinch tightening.

With all of that said, how do we determine what makes a good saddle for *your* horse? Let's examine the foundation of the saddle—the TREE.

Quality of the finished saddle begins with a saddle tree. But remember, a superior quality tree does not guarantee a high quality saddle. However, a poor quality tree will result in a low grade saddle regardless of how beautiful it is on the outside. Keep in mind, a garbage truck with a Charles Russell painting on its side still smells like a garbage truck!

Currently, most saddle trees are made of wood with a rawhide cover. There are also trees made of wood with a fiberglass coating and trees made of molded plastic. Some trees are made of wood and covered with canvas. A recent innovation is a tree made of aluminum. And, there are trees made of hollow fiberglass. Synthetic trees have their own set of problems, which include poor design and inability to hold nails and screws securely.

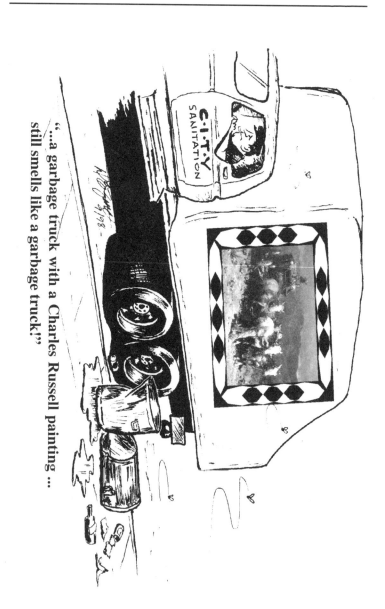

"...a garbage truck with a Charles Russell painting ... still smells like a garbage truck!"

Saddle trees only have five parts: the two bars, the fork, the horn and the cantle. Each of these parts is very important to the look and the function of the finished saddle, but most important for the horse are the bars.

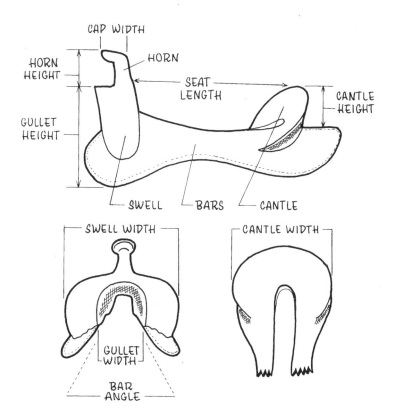

The BARS are the parts that rest on the horse's back. This is the actual bearing surface of the saddle. There is a left and a right and there are a number of styles to consider. The four basic bar types are:

(1)*Regular*, or standard, bars with double grooves for the stirrup leathers to be recessed into, are used on most trees

(2)*Northwest* bars are little wider, giving more of a bearing surface. They also have double grooves for the stirrup leathers

(3)*Arizona* bars are very strong, give good support and are identified by having only one stirrup leather groove

(4) *Arabian* bars are slightly shorter because the Arabian horse has one less vertebrae. They can be made with any of the above styles.

BARS

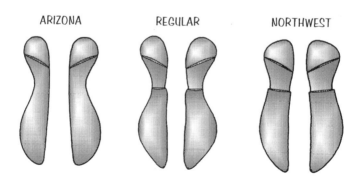

ARIZONA   REGULAR   NORTHWEST

The bar lengths sometimes vary because of different seat lengths. The proper length of the bars has been a subject of much discussion for many generations. One theory is that a long bar distributes the weight of the rider over a greater area of the back, while another theory is that long bars tend to gall the horse at their rearmost end and that the shorter bar distributes the weight to be correctly supported by the horse's bone and muscle structure. In spite of recent discussion on saddle fitting, there has been little research on the effects of different length bars. What is most important is the weight be evenly distributed across the horse's back and not cause any pressure on the kidneys and loins.

These bars, like the rest of the tree, are constructed of white Ponderosa Pine, Beachwood or Ash. Sometimes Laurel, Willow or Douglas fir are used. Hardwoods have been found unsatisfactory due to their tendency to crack and split. The softer woods have more flexibility and do not split and crack as easily. The bars are usually made of one piece, though sometimes they are laminated.

These bars are not flat. They have a contour and a twist (known as the "rocker") in their shape. The bars are more rounded under the swells and are broader and flatter on the surface beneath the cantle. This

---

contour accommodates the depression in the back of
most horses. What we're trying to accomplish here is
a wider distribution of weight over the entire surface.

Let's talk about weight distribution for a moment. For
purposes of discussion, we will assume that our rider
weighs 150 pounds. A typical Western saddle will have
a total bearing surface [under the bars only, with no
regard to the skirts] of approximately 185 square
inches. With the 150 pound rider on board, this typical
Western saddle will only be applying slightly more than
3/4 of a pound per square inch to our horse's back. Of
course, these numbers will change somewhat
depending upon the rider's weight and the weight of
the saddle. It is easy to see why weight distribution is
an important factor in the design of the saddle.

By contrast, an English saddle rests only on its bars
and has no skirts to further distribute weight. The
typical English saddle will have a total bearing surface
of about 86 square inches. This means that the bearing
surface is carrying approximately 1 3/4 pounds per
square inch. This is very good because studies have
shown that weight in excess of 2.8 pounds per square
inch will cause pressure sores and should be the
maximum per square inch weight applied to a horse's
back.

While we're discussing weight, I would like to point

out another common misconception. I see many riders today who are overly concerned about adding a few pounds to their rig. When a rider asks me "How much do your saddles weigh?" and I answer, "34 to 38 pounds", the usual response is that they feel it is quite important for the saddle to weigh six or eight pounds less! I have been told by these same riders that six pounds will make a big difference in the performance of their horse as the day wears on.

Again, let's evaluate some weight distribution as we did with the saddletree. Keep in mind, as I compare weight on the back of a person and weight on the back of a horse that a horse's physical structure is so designed *to carry more weight in proportion to its body* than a human being can carry in proportion to their body. Six pounds to a one hundred fifty pound person is .04 of their total body weight while six pounds to an eleven hundred pound horse is .005 of its total body weight. In other words, *six pounds* will cause less stress to the horse than eleven ounces would cause to a person carrying this weight in a backpack! I enjoy teasing riders who are concerned about 6 pounds of weight by telling them that if it's that important they should either go on a diet ... or leave their boots at home!

Consider the amount of weight a pack horse carries, [much more than the weight of a man and saddle] with no ill effect ... providing the pack is *balanced*.

An important part of the fork dimension is the *gullet*.
This is the cutout, or tunnel, underneath the center of
the fork and is positioned directly over the withers of
the horse. It is absolutely important that the height of
the gullet provides plenty of clearance above the
withers. If the gullet is too short it will rub the horse
raw on top of his withers. If the gullet is too wide
[i.e.; a full quarter horse tree on a horse that should use
a semi-quarter horse tree] it will allow the saddle to sit
too low on the withers and will cause the same problem
as a gullet that is made too short. A good rule to use
when trying to judge the proper height on your horse
is "two fingers clearance". Place your saddle on the
back of the horse without using any kind of pad or
saddle blanket and determine if there's clearance for
two fingers between your horse's withers and the gullet.

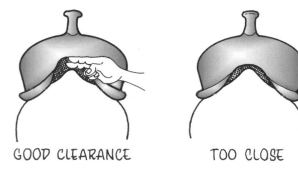

GOOD CLEARANCE   TOO CLOSE

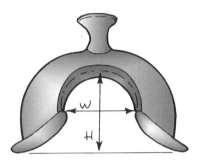

MEASURING THE
—— GULLET ——

W

H

The *width* of the gullet is measured straight across from the point where the bars join the fork to the same point on the opposite side. (We have already discussed the width of the gullet based upon regular, semi-quarter horse and full-quarter horse bars.) The *height* of the gullet is measured when the tree bars are resting on a flat surface. The average height of the gullet on a Western saddle is between 7 1/2 and 8 inches high. Occasionally a gullet is made 9 or 9 1/2 inches high, but this is unusual. A gullet above this height would mean that the fork must be made taller and would increase the leverage applied to the front of the bars if this saddle was used for roping. I would strongly suggest that if a horse requires this additional gullet height he probably is not suited to be a good roping prospect.

The way these bars set on horse's back, high or low, is controlled by the width of the gullet [the arch under the fork]. There are generally only four different gullet widths used to fit the withers and backs of various sized horses.

    1. Regular   5 3/4"
    2. Semi-quarter horse   6 1/4"
    3. Quarter horse   6 1/2"
    4. Extra-wide Quarter horse 6 3/4"

All of these widths are built with the same angle at the front, except the quarter-horse widths, which have a flatter angle to the bars.

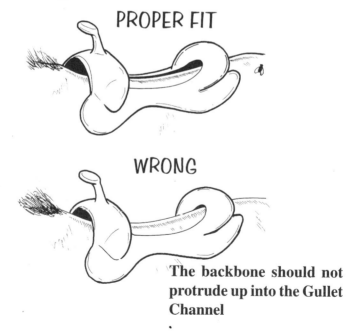

PROPER FIT

WRONG

The backbone should not protrude up into the Gullet Channel

Because the gullet effects areas of pressure on the horse's back, it definitely must be correct. It is very difficult to measure the gullet after the saddle has been constructed. The leather on the gullet and sheepskin on the skirts can prevent you from getting a good measurement. The best test is to place the saddle on your horse's back. Slight differences in bar angle and rocker can be compensated for with good pads. I will discuss pads and blankets later in this book.

Something else to keep in mind when buying a saddle is the the appearance of the fork and gullet in relationship to the rest of the saddle. In other words, you wouldn't want a low Association style fork with a 6" cantle nor would you want a high fork style, or swept back style, with a very low cantle.

If the saddle is intended to be used for cutting horses, the bar shape should be much narrower in the mid-bar area to provide for greater leg contact with the horse. However, this weakens the saddle and it should never be used for roping.

Most horses today fall in the range of nine hundred to twelve hundred pounds and the semi-quarter horse gullet width fits them quite well. Keep this in mind when you ask a saddlemaker to rebuild an old family heirloom saddle. It will probably be too narrow to use on today's horses.

Rather than trying to restore the old saddle to use, you would be better off having the old tree duplicated with modern bars. The old bars are probably not only too close together in the gullet, but are also too straight without enough rocker in them. Today's horses are bred for bigger backs and they're better nourished and their general health is better which helps them develop better muscling. The *rocker* in the bar is to conform to the sway in a horse's back and the *flare* is the flatter angle at the back which is done so no sharp edges will dig into the horse. The *twist* allows the rocker and flare to make the angle transitions between the withers and loin area.

The gap between the bars is known as the *gullet groove* and its purpose is to relieve pressure from the horse's backbone. This gap keeps any weight and friction off the backbone. Bars that are either thin or set too wide at the gullet place the tree too low on the horse's back and the groundseat will rub the backbone raw. Bars that are extra wide, or set too narrow at the gullet, will make the saddle ride high on the horse and be very unstable feeling. This narrow setting will cause the bottom edge of the bars to dig into the animal's back. These pressure points will cause the distribution of weight per square inch to change in a very negative manner.

It is very difficult to assess the fit of the tree when the saddle is fully constructed with heavy skirting leather and sheepskin, however, by merely placing the saddletree on the horse's back with no blanket or pad you can make a fair evaluation. If the backbone sticks up into the gullet groove the saddle is probably too wide. Another indication would be lack of clearance over the withers under the gullet [unless the horse has very high withers, which would require a special tree with a higher than normal gullet]. A good quality saddle pad will help make the average tree fit your horse very well. The saddle pad also helps distribute weight to some small degree.

A saddle pad will not make up for a BAD fitting saddle, but it will make your average saddle fit like a glove. As an example of this think about a backpack for yourself — we all use the same size backpack, however, we make it fit us comfortably through the adjustment of the pads and padding on the straps. A backpack is a frame to distribute weight just the same as a saddle tree is a frame to distribute weight. The padding makes my backpack fit me well and it can fit you well, too, with minor adjustments.

At this point you're asking yourself, "What size saddle should I get for my horse? Where should I begin?" Well, I find that most horses get along fine with the semi-quarter horse width, Arizona style bars.

Over the years I have found this to be satisfactory for approximately 85% of the horses I have been acquainted with, from ranches and back yards to livery stables.

You've no doubt heard many people speak of bending a heavy wire over the horse's back to determine the shape of a tree. This is only practical as a means to determine if the tree fits within *acceptable limits*. This may not be a bad idea if you feel your horse's back is quite unusual. (However, remember if it is that unusual you will not be able to use this saddle on any other horse) The proper way to use this method is to carefully bend a heavy wire [usually a copper wire works best] over the horse's withers and trace that pattern onto a large piece of paper or cardboard, then do the same thing over the mid-back for the center of the bars and further back where rear edge of the bars will set. Trace all three of these outlines on cardboard, cut out the outline and hold these pieces up under the tree bars to compare with the bare tree that your saddlemaker is going to use on your horse. This will show you if the tree will fit closely. Don't forget what was said earlier about changing conformation and the use of good quality pads to obtain that "perfect" fit.

The FORK is the front of the saddle and controls the gullet width. It is called the fork because in the old days the saddlemaker created this part of the saddle from the fork of a tree. The horn and the fork were cut from one piece of wood. The style of the fork went through a great evolutionary period because of the many uses that riders created for their saddles . (By the way, the word *pommel* is generally used with English saddles and the words *fork* or *swell* apply to Western saddles.)

Over the years riders found that if the outsides of the fork were extended wider than the attachment place to the bar they could get a better hold with their knees will riding a bronc. This was a good idea, but like all good ideas, got carried too far. Some say saddlemakers were asked to make forks as wide as 24 inches! Any saddle with an extreme measurement like this is known in the trade as a "freak". A typical saddle of this type was the "bear trap". This tree has a very wide swell and the swells were turned backward at a strong angle from the horn so that the rider was literally in a trap between the old high-back cantle and the fork. It really did a good job of holding the bronco-buster on top of the horse, but it was almost impossible to get out of if the horse fell. A saddle of this style is commonly considered to be very dangerous. These are fun to look at and collect, but, please be careful if you ride one.

There are hundreds of fork styles, however, they'll generally fall into two classes — *A-fork (or slick fork)* and *swell fork*. An A-fork typically is smooth, or straight down, on the outside from the horn to the bars. The swell fork is wider and thicker from side to side and may even be *undercut*. A roping saddle will have a swell fork with no undercut.

Ropers do not prefer swells too wide or undercut because the rope can catch under the edges of the fork and cause unnecessary pressures on the horse's back. Professional ropers also disliked the wide swell saddles because they cut down the speed of their dismount.

The name of any particular tree is derived from the style of the fork, a fork pattern that was used or designed by the individual whose name is now associated with this style. The bars, the horn and the cantle may all be quite different on an S.F. Bowman tree [as an example] but if it's a Bowman fork the tree is called a Bowman. The names and styles of trees will vary from one part of the country to the next, however, most treemakers can cross reference with the manufacturers of other saddle trees and make exactly what you want. It is very interesting to study a treemaker's catalog to see the variety that they offer. There are literally hundreds of different fork styles available.

Forks can be attached to the bars at different angles. A slight slope from the bars to the top of the fork is considered *straight up*. When the angle begins to lean

FORKS

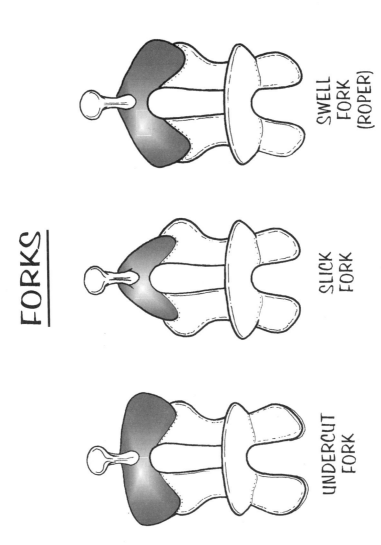

SWELL
FORK
(ROPER)

SLICK
FORK

UNDERCUT
FORK

FORKS SHOWING DIFFERENT SLOPES

STRAIGHT UP

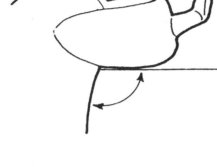

MEDIUM SLOPE

FULL SLOPE

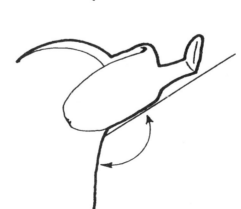

forward it is considered a *medium slope* fork and if the angle is increased a few more degrees it is considered a *full slope* fork. This fork angle has little to do with the fit of the tree and does not affect your comfort until we get into the full slope fork. The full slope fork is rarely seen today. It was quite common in saddles of the 1950's, however, riders who need more space in the seat might find this to be a useful design.

The HORN comes in a wide range of shapes and sizes. It sits on top of the gullet and is one of the most identifiable elements of the Western saddle. The shapes and sizes are dictated by both usage and style. Horns are used as a snubbing post for a rope; a convenient hook for halters, bridles, binoculars and lunch boxes; a handhold for when the riding gets rough; a convenient spot to lean on while watching the sun set; and for some, a spot to apply some silver.

Most horns are made from bronze, steel or solid wood. When the horn is made of metal it is countersunk and bolted into the fork before the rawhide cover is sewn on. This makes it a solid part of the tree, forming a complete unit, and ready to take all stresses. When the horn is made of wood it is carved with the fork from the same piece of wood or laminate to give it a great deal of strength. Post style horns are always wood.

HOW TO MEASURE A HORN

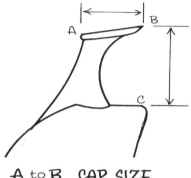

A to B   CAP SIZE
B to C   HORN HEIGHT

Horns were developed originally for roping. The two types of ropers are the *dally* ropers and the *hard-and-fast-tie* ropers. The dally roper snubs his lariat around the horn one or two times in a half hitch and then plays it out to absorb much of the shock as the steer hits the end of the rope. (This is similar to fly fishing except the "string" is attached to a half-ton bovine and the rider can be the one doing the flying!) With calf ropers, the style is to cast the loop at the calf and as it goes over his head take a fast turn or two around the horn. The common joke, though not so funny, is that you can tell when a cowboy is a dally roper by the number of fingers missing from his hand.

Hard-and-fast tie ropers work with their lariat securely tied to the horn at all times. This was a common practice with riders who worked in heavy brush country. When their string dropped on a target they didn't want to take a chance of losing it. (Many times this method proved that they hadn't checked the strength of their cinches and they were treated to the sight of a steer leaving the country with a saddle following along in the dust.)

Horns are attached to the swells with screws and bolts. Most metal horns have either four prong bases or a steel plate with four holes in the base. These usually have a combination of both screws and bolts to ensure their security to the top of the fork. For even more security a horn can be bolted to a steel plate under the gullet. After being bolted to the fork, the horn is covered with rawhide for additional strength and to make it to an integral part of the tree. Horns may be ordered in any combination of height, cap size or angle. When choosing the horn for your saddle remember that the leather wrapping will increase the diameter of the neck and <u>leather covered</u> horn caps will finish out almost one inch larger in diameter. A finished <u>rawhide cover</u> will be about one half inch larger. Many saddles horns are wrapped around the neck for extra strength and durability. This wrapping may be made of latigo or "mulehide", a rough-out, gray colored leather.

The raised portion at the rear of the seat is called the CANTLE. This cantle bridges the bars at the back of the saddle and secures their angle and width in place properly. It also gives the rider a comfortable support to lean against during long rides and even when the horse is just standing still. Early saddles had very high cantles. Most of these were in the five to six inch range. Looking over old photos of Western saddles it appears that some time in the early 1920's the height of the cantle began to lower. In the late 1950's and early 1960's cantles shrunk down as low is 2 inches. This was only a fad of the time and riders found it very difficult to remain seated when a horse bolted forward proving, once again, that saddle parts aren't just for looks.

I've often been told that a roper wants to dismount quickly from his horse and needs the least obstruction from the cantle that he can get. Some ropers exclaim that any cantle over three inches is just in their way. After reviewing many videos, it's been proven that when the cowboy swings off after roping a calf, his leg clears the saddle by six to eight inches. This leaves a lot of room to spare if you have a 4 or 4 1/2" cantle. The advantage to the deeper seat is the roping improves immediately because when the horse leaps out of the box the rider is able to move with him rather than fighting to stay in the saddle.

A deep seat [one with a 5 inch or taller cantle] has many advantages. It provides a great deal of back support which makes for a more comfortable long ride. It holds the rider in place better and, therefore, cuts down on excess movement on the horse's back. Less movement means a more comfortable horse, as too much wiggling in the saddle may cause sores. The taller cantle also keeps the rider from sitting too high in the saddle which would cause undue pressure on the horse's kidneys by leveraging the tree bars downward. Another advantage of the high cantle is that it's helpful in keeping the pressure off the riders thighs when leading another horse or dragging a cow with the lariat.

Just like the fork, cantles can be attached to the bars with varying pitches or slopes. There is a *low-sloped* cantle, a *medium-sloped* cantle and a *steep-slope* cantle. The height of the cantle is measured on the back side from the bars to the highest center point. They're usually ordered in one-half inch increments. Cantles also come in various widths; 12 to 13 inches being the most common.

The same cantle can look quite different from one saddle to another due to the amount of "dish" or hollowing out it has and the type of cantle-binding used to finish it.

CANTLE SLOPE OR PITCH

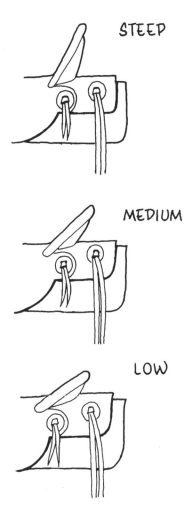

STEEP

MEDIUM

LOW

There are many different types of cantles being used today, but the most common styles are:

1 - REGULAR — This is the most common cantle today. It is usually three to four inches high and has a full, graceful curve across the top.

2 - COMFORT — Has round sides and a flat top. It retains the side support for the riders hips without applying pressure to lower back as a higher cantle does. It gives little of the support that is necessary in the saddle and tends to dig into the flesh of "wider" riders. [Who named this thing "comfort" in the first place?]

3 - SHOVEL — A style commonly used at the turn of the century. Sometimes it has a beveled edge to relieve the pressure against hips. It is usually 5 to 6 inches high and never wider than 12 inches. The dish, if any, is never more than 1/2 inch. (Those old-time cowboys were tough!)

The *dish* in a cantle is the depth of the recess from the front. The common measurement is 1 to 1 1/2 half inches, though there are some as deep as two inches. This dish determines how deeply you will sit back in the seat and how well it will match your own shape. Too shallow and it will feel as though you're sitting against a flat board and too deep a dish will cause undue pressure against the edges of your own "sitting parts".

When ordering a saddle it is rare that you will be asked
how much dish you require. Most competent
saddlemakers and treemakers will automatically cut
the appropriate amount of dish to correspond to the
cantle you have requested. If saddles have always been
uncomfortable in this area for you be sure to discuss it
with your saddlemaker. As little as 1/4 inch more or
less dish can make a big difference.

CANTLE SHAPES

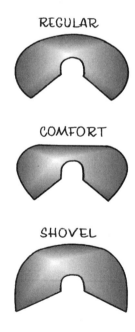

REGULAR

COMFORT

SHOVEL

The <u>seat length</u> is controlled by the position of the cantle. To determine the size of the seat, measure from the base of the horn to the top center of the cantle. A typical length is 15 1/2 inches with the average bar length 22 to 23 inches. This would leave 3 inches of the bar behind the cantle providing good weight distribution of the rider. With shorter seats the bars must be shortened accordingly and the same is true for longer seats. However, we must also be careful that the bars never exceed 24 inches in length. If the bars are too long, and a heavy rider sits too far back, great discomfort is caused to the horse and his movements will be restricted. It is my opinion that no saddle should be made with a larger seat size than 17 inches. This will leave only 2 1/2 inches of bar beyond a cantle. Any seat longer than this, with 24 inch bars, simply applies too much pressure to a horse's loins and kidneys. If a larger seat is required the rider should choose a horse more in the draft family and have a custom tree made to accommodate his needs.

The assembly of these parts is our next consideration. I'm sure you'll be amazed to find that most of these parts, in even the best of trees, are put together with staples and small nails, not the big 3/8 inch lag bolts you would imagine. Wood putty is also used to smooth surfaces and create nice contours at the base of the fork. The small fasteners and modern glues are strong enough to hold the pieces in place as the rawhide covering dries and shrinks.

Rawhide is the untanned hide of an animal. For saddles, de-haired cowhide is used. Rawhide is worked wet and is fit and stitched to completely encase all of the parts of the tree. The best results, and strongest trees, are obtained when the rawhide has never been dried out between the time the animal was slaughtered and when it is applied to the tree, not dried and rewet. The seams are laced with *deer rawhide* strings on the best quality trees, while cheaper trees are laced with nylon or cotton cord. On the concave surfaces [gullet, cantle face, etc.] the rawhide is nailed to the wooden tree to help it retain its shape during the drying process.

The tree is then set aside to be dried slowly and under carefully monitored conditions. It must be clamped down to a strong, flat surface to prevent it from warping as it dries. After the drying process is completed, the tree is sealed with heavy coats of varnish to prevent moisture from getting to the rawhide.

A few manufacturers offer both heavy and light weight rawhide covers. Many of them refer to their rawhide as a "bullhide". However, this is a trade name for the heaviest rawhide covering and has nothing to do with the sex of the animal. After all, most beef cattle that go to market are steers and cows with very few bulls going to slaughter "intact". All leathers starts at the beef packing plant's slaughter house and goes from there to the tanneries. The buyers for the tanneries are concerned with the quality of the hide and give little consideration to the gender of the animal.

Some shops offer "double bullhide covers" and claim that this will add a great deal of strength to your saddle. There have been no good studies that actually prove any strength gain from double rawhide covering. It is my opinion that the only thing to be gained with double covering a tree is a heavier tree and a lighter wallet.

In the course of this discussion about trees I must offer my opinion of the saddle shops that lay claim to making their own trees. A few makers offer this service with the announcement that their saddles are truly "custom all the way". My opinion is that if this person can really make a tree which is better than all others, is he not purely selfish because he will not share this design with the horse world and, perhaps, license his design to one of the large tree making shops for the benefit of all? If his design isn't that unique he can purchase an exceptionally well made tree from a treemaking company (a separate art onto itself) for a very reasonable fee. The time of any saddlemaker, who's work is of good quality, is far too valuable to divide that time on the job of treemaking. Saddlemakers are tooled-up to do leatherwork.

Treemakers are tooled-up to do woodwork. Even if
the saddlemaker was prepared to make the trees
himself, he cannot make enough trees in a year to keep
his skills honed to the same level as a full time tree
maker.

At this point you're asking yourself, "What about other
materials — like fiberglass?". Well, you're right,
there are trees made of fiberglass. There are also
wooden trees that are covered with canvas and shellac.
I don't think much of of either one. They're lower
priced alternatives to the real thing. Casting fiberglass
is very economical. It is the least expensive way to
make a saddle tree. However, once the molds are made,
that is the size and the shape of that model forever. It
cannot be adjusted for differences required by many
horses and riders and you end up with a "cookie cutter"
saddle which usually fits all riders and horses equally.
Equally bad, that is! Often these fiberglass trees can
weigh more than a good quality wood and rawhide
tree.

In order to make a "universal size", usually the bars
are too short, the width of the bars too narrow in the
back, the shoulder pads too small, the seat too flat and
the steel horns are cast in place with a single rod down
in the fork [which has very little strength]. Most
saddlemakers find these fiberglass trees will not hold
a nail or screw as well as a wooden tree during the

construction process and are, therefore, not considered a very safe saddle foundation.

Synthetic [plastic] trees entered the market in 1964 and today are used in a major proportion of all saddles manufactured in the United States. They are available in many styles and are used by saddle factories because of identical size, shape, and uniformity. They are ideal for use when mass producing saddles. They are also very attractive to saddle manufacturers due to their cost, which is about 75 percent less than a high-quality, rawhide covered tree. Custom saddles can be built on these trees but you must be willing to accept their specifications and limitations. Due to their abbreviated bar length and width they cannot offer the same amount of weight distribution as a wooden tree and they don't seem to be as strong under most conditions. If you have a saddle built on a tree of this type you should expect to pay considerably less for the finished product. You can also be assured that it will never be the same high quality as a custom made saddle on a rawhide tree.

I must mention one more type of tree. A recent development is the fiberglass covered, hand carved wooden tree. There are a few companies now offering this variation on the saddle tree. If the fiberglass is applied skillfully, and not just a "plastic" solution poured over the tree, it could be a good alternative to rawhide. This is a new process and has not been thoroughly tested by time and use. Before deciding to use a tree of this type it would be wise to check with other riders who have had experience with them.

Because there is no standardization among the treemakers, I cannot give you anything as an exact set of ideal measurements for a tree or for any particular situation. There is no such thing as a "best" bar name. As stated before, I prefer the semi-quarter horse bars. However, the fork, horn and cantle are entirely up to you. When you order a saddle from a custom maker, ask his advice and listen carefully. He not only wants to please you but he also wants to make a saddle that will be a credit to his reputation and not some sort of "freak" rig that is a new rider's attempt to be clever.

I cannot over-emphasize the importance of selecting your tree carefully. You don't have to be an expert horseman, but you do need to determine what use you will put the saddle to and what kind of horses you will ride most frequently.

A good saddle should last the rest of your life. Choose it carefully and enjoy the ride!

GROUND SEAT

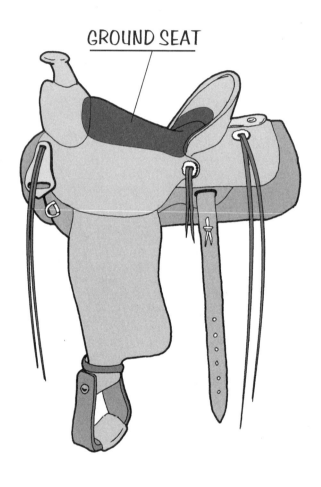

GROUND SEAT

The ground seat is one of the most important parts of the saddle. The ground seat is beneath the leather cover of the seat and it is almost impossible to see any of its components. The only areas of it that are visible are viewed through the hand hole and underneath in the "gullet channel". I have seen people pull up the side jockeys in an attempt to view portions of the ground seat, however, if the ground seat leather is properly tapered no construction can be evaluated by looking under the seat jockey. Trying to look under the seat jockey to "see how it's built" only displays a complete lack of knowledge about saddle construction.

The reason the ground seat is so important is that its shape will determine where you sit on the horse's back and how comfortable your ride will be. If the ground seat is not properly formed the saddle will only be comfortable for short rides, and, even then, can cause back aches, leg pain and sore hips. Your new saddle may be the best looking rig in the world, but if it is not comfortable you don't have a good saddle. All of the parts are very important, but the seat is what you will feel continuously and if it is uncomfortable it will certainly turn an otherwise enjoyable ride into a painful or bad experience.

There several things to consider when evaluating the ground seat. Sit in your favorite easy chair. It is very flat and deeply padded. This padding rises to form a pocket which gives support and allows you to sit for long periods of time with a good degree of comfort. The rear of this "easy chair" supports your back and relieves some of the strain against your hips while the back side of your upper thighs also carry some of the weight. The only way that this relates to the way you sit in a saddle is the position of your back. If you lean forward in the seat you apply stresses to your lower backbone. When you sit up straight and allow the rear of the chair to support your back it relieves some of the pressure from your hips and pelvis.

When sitting on the saddle most of your body weight rests on your hips and is transferred to your lower pelvic bones. The inside of your thighs and your knees will carry some of your weight, however, only a small proportion. With all of this weight concentrated on your pelvic bones the shaping of the ground seat is extremely important. The ground seat must be carved to match the *pelvic arch*. It should have a gentle curve across the seat to give firm, yet gentle, support to the "fleshier" portions of your sitting anatomy. If the arch is too high, it will be like straddling a fence rail and would become extremely painful in a short time. If the arch is too low, (or nonexistent and flat as in many saddles today) it will make you feel as though you are riding astride a park bench in a short time. A flat seat is no different than sitting on a 2x8 piece of lumber. Eventually all of your weight will be carried by the points of your pelvic bones and will make you marvel at the endurance of the old cowboys who rode across the Great Plains.

The arching across the seat is only slight, as seen in the illustration, but it is absolutely essential to a comfortable seat. If this ground work is not done correctly no amount of padding that will make the saddle right for longer rides.

This arch is the same for a man's saddle as well as a woman's saddle. The pelvic bones may contact the seat at a wider position, but the principles are the same. The only difference that should be observed is the width adjustment for extremely large or small individuals.

A properly constructed groundseat has this arching and also is carved narrow near the front to create a natural position for the thighs to rest in. This aids in seating position and closeness to the horse.

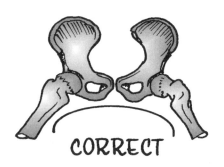

CORRECT

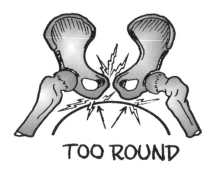

TOO ROUND

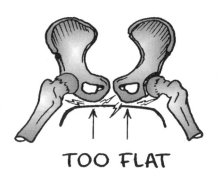

TOO FLAT

The cantle should be sufficiently tall to give some support to your back. How does this work? If the cantle is at least 4" high and has the proper dish it will support the back of your pelvis and prevent it from rotating to the rear. This, in turn, relieves muscular pressure from your hips and takes stress away from the backbone and back muscles.

Also of great importance in the ground seat is the *slope*. This will determine where you sit, front or back, in the saddle. The slope begins at the handhold and gracefully curves down to the front of the cantle. The slope, or "rise", determines how much room is in the seat and how narrow the saddle feels. A high rise can make a big seat feel quite small by forcing the rider back too close to the cantle. A low rise makes the saddle feel much larger, however, it may allow the rider too much front-to-back movement.

A well made ground seat can be as thick as 1" or more at the hand hole but should be as thin as possible toward the rear of the saddle for the rider to sit as close as can be to the horse. Remember, if the ground seat forces you up and away from your tree that also moves you higher above the horse. It is important that your saddle allow you to sit close to the horse to keep your center of gravity low.

SEAT SLOPES

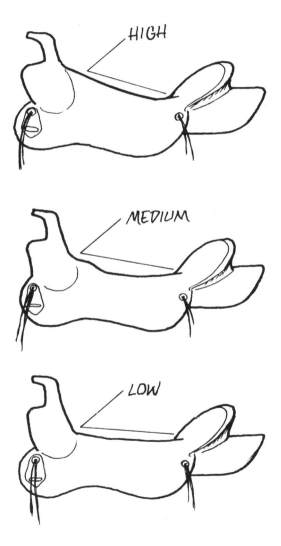

There are many different ways to make a ground seat. The most common is the metal/leather style. This consists of galvanized tin strainer plates covered with a number of pieces of leather. The strainer plate may be made of either one or two pieces of metal. The bottom is covered with a light weight piece of leather for cosmetic purposes only. This is visible when looking under the saddle at the gullet channel. By the way, this is called the strainer plate because it is nailed along the bars of the tree and relieves some of the pressure, or strain, applied to the tree.

On top of the strainer plate are additional pieces of leather which are glued in place and carefully shaped and carved until this ground seat meets the requirements of the rider and the saddlemaker.

GROUND SEAT

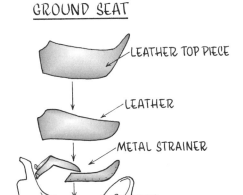

LEATHER TOP PIECE

LEATHER

METAL STRAINER

The number of pieces applied may vary from two to five depending upon the rise needed and the thickness of leather used. The shaping of the ground seat requires an experienced hand and a good eye for symmetry and uniformity. The saddlemaker must be both an engineer and artist. The overall shape and lines should flow together smoothly and gracefully. If you are having a custom saddle made ask to sit in the ground seat before any further work is done. This will tell you a great deal about the feel of the finished saddle.

The all-leather ground seat is, as the name implies, made entirely of leather with no metal strainer piece employed. It is created by gluing a number of wet pieces of leather together and, with the use of a wedge, allowing it to dry in the desired shape. The finished product is then very hard and solid, much like the heel of boot. After drying this is shaped and carved in the same manner as described above. This can be an excellent foundation when created by an experienced craftsmen, but can be a nightmare when not made properly.

Many horsemen make the claim that the "only good ground seat is the all-leather ground seat". They also maintain that any metal strainer is uncomfortable and a cheap way to build a saddle. Both of these statements are untrue and usually show a great deal of ignorance on the part of the speaker. I believe that the two piece tin strainer is by far the most superior method. My reason is that the two-piece creates exactly the same arched shape that is found in the all leather ground seat and, as an added bonus, also provides much greater strength for maintaining the shape throughout the life of the saddle. The front piece of the strainer plate is forged into the classic Gothic arch which is one of the strongest architectural shapes known.

After leather is removed from the forward edges of the ground seat to allow stirrup leathers to pass over the tree bars the all leather ground seat is weakened somewhat. The tin strainer, in particular the two piece tin strainer, affords greater strength in this area.

The one-piece metal strainer is also good, but it does not afford the rise in the front without a considerable buildup of leather. It also requires thick leather underneath (called "risers") to afford clearance for the stirrup leathers. It is easiest to make, and therefore, the most commonly used.

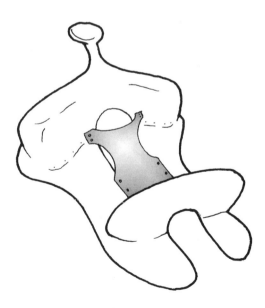

Criticism of the metal/leather ground seat should be
directed at the person building the saddle rather than
the technique used.

A popular strainer in use today is made of fiberglass.
It looks and functions like the tin strainer but is cheaper
and can be applied faster. It is not fully shaped and
creates a "flat" seat basis. This flat seat is similar to
sitting on a 2x6 board. Not very comfortable! Price
and speed are the reasons that the strainer is used by
factories and production shops. I can't believe that
any quality saddlemaker would make use of this type
of strainer.

Because most manufactured saddles today are made
with fiberglass trees there is no control of the ground
seat shapes by the maker. The ground seat is already
cast into the trees and close observation will show
you this seat is always flat just in front of the cantle.
This makes for an uncomfortable ride because it's back
to riding on that 2x6 flat board! No saddlemaker
interested in quality will create such a ride.

Remember that you cannot see how the ground seat is
built without disassembling the saddle and you must
rely upon the maker and your own good judgment. To
evaluate the ground seat, carefully look over the shape
and the gracefulness of the seat and, finally, sit in the
saddle. Just sit there quietly with your arms folded

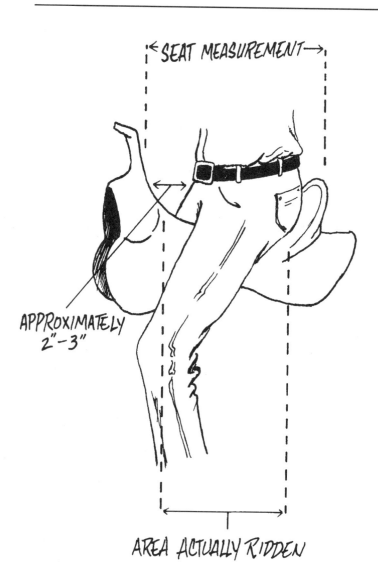

SEAT MEASUREMENT

APPROXIMATELY
2"–3"

AREA ACTUALLY RIDDEN

and concentrate on the feel. Move back and forth, but only slightly, to look for ridges and lumps that might show themselves after an hour's ride.

Is it comfortable in the base? How about the cantle area? Does it "hold" you in place? Is the cantle digging into your belt? There should be a natural feel to the position your thighs are in ... not too wide, but with some support. (Don't look for it to be too narrow. Remember, it can only be as narrow as the horse's back.) There should also be a couple of inches between your thighs and the bottom of the fork edges.

You've heard the expression "no hoof, no horse", now you can have the expression "no seat, no saddle".

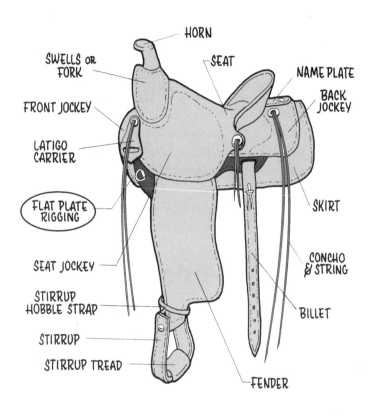

HORN

SWELLS OR FORK

SEAT

NAME PLATE

BACK JOCKEY

FRONT JOCKEY

LATIGO CARRIER

FLAT PLATE RIGGING

SKIRT

SEAT JOCKEY

CONCHO & STRING

STIRRUP HOBBLE STRAP

BILLET

STIRRUP

STIRRUP TREAD

FENDER

RIGGINGS

The styles of *riggings* and their relative positions are one of the most misunderstood parts of the saddle. Just as the style of the ground seat determines where and how you will sit on a saddle the rigging dictates where and how the saddle will sit on the horse's back. The rigging is also the most important part of the saddle affecting your safety. Those parts of the saddle known as the riggings are truly an arrangement of rings and plates that provide anchor points for the latigos and tie straps which hold the saddle safely and securely on the animals back.

Rigging hardware may be attached directly to the tree or built into the skirts. When only a front rigging is installed, the saddle is called a *single rig* outfit. When a provision is made to install a rear cinch the saddle is then called a *double rig*.

When mankind started to ride horses a surcingle was used. This was generally a wide strap fastened around the horse's girth just behind his front legs. When a framework (the tree) began to be used this surcingle held that framework in place and was the first cinch rigging. It was considered inadequate in a short time because the tree often slid from side to side and it was difficult to keep in place during hard riding. Eventually someone thought to fasten this strap arrangement to the tree, and from that many styles and positions of rigging have evolved.

In the early days, when horses were first introduced to the Americas, the predominant rigging style used by the Spanish in California was a strap over the front of the fork with a ring attached on each side and another strap secured to the back of the saddle behind the cantle. This was known as the *Spanish rigging* and the ring was in the position we call "full". This was later replaced by the *centerfire* rigging also known as the *California rigging*.

The riders in California were mostly dally ropers and that style of roping never created the hard pull on the saddle that occurs with the hard-and-fast-tie roping style used by Texans. This rig was used primarily in flat country and was not designed for heavy roping. It was also best used on a horse with good withers, a narrow back and with a wide cinch. The Texas roper used a shorter rope that was tied securely to the saddle horn. When a cow hit the end of the rope, it gave a violent jerk to the saddle. Because the full rigging was directly under the fork of the tree a pivot point was created and the rear of the saddle would tilt upward under this terrific strain. To keep the saddle from tilting upward, a second cinch, known as the *flank cinch*, was added to the back. The evolution from full-double to the seven-eighths double and then the three-quarter double rig was only a short step.

One of the earliest rigging styles, commonly seen on the Great Plains saddles, is the Sam Stagg rigging. This is a very interesting rigging which seems to have been prevalent around 1880.

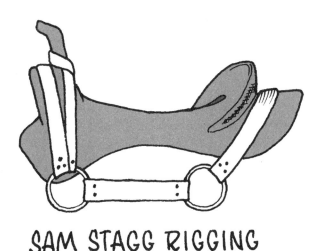

SAM STAGG RIGGING

With this style rigging the front ring is usually at the full position and only rarely found in the seven-eights position. The front rings were held in place by two straps. The first strap was riveted to the ring on the left and went over the front of the fork to the ring on the right. The second strap went from left to right, however, it wrapped around the horn from the back side and down to the other side. (This was to prevent the rings from sliding up and down) The rear rings were secured by a shaped strap cut to follow the curve of the cantle, sometimes laced in the middle. The front and back rings were fastened to each other with a short one inch strap. This entire arrangement was very much like a harness which was then slipped over the top of the saddle and set down to hold the saddle in place. It was not usually fastened firmly to the tree.

The positions of the rigging are easily determined by looking at the accompanying chart. Full position is directly under the center of the fork. Center fire is the halfway point between the fork and the cantle. To determine three-quarters position find centerfire and full and mark the central point between these two. To mark seven-eighths simply divide full position and three quarter position. These name designations for the positions apply to all rigging styles, types and materials.

RIGGING POSITIONS

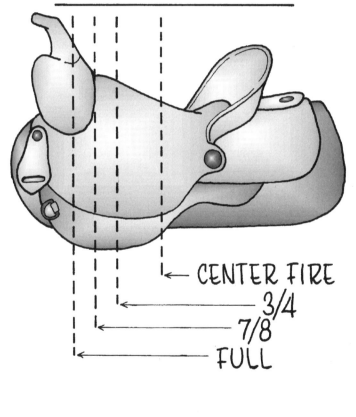

← CENTER FIRE
3/4
7/8
FULL

RIGGING POSITIONS

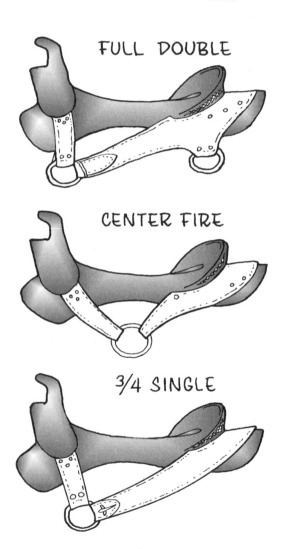

FULL DOUBLE

CENTER FIRE

3/4 SINGLE

Today's riggings are fastened much more securely. Most saddlemakers secure the rings to the leather with rivets or lace or a combination of both. The leather is then fastened to the tree with a combination of screws and nails. The rigging must be fastened extremely securely for safety. Screws and nails driven into a rawhide covered, wooden tree are quite safe, however, I have never seen these fasteners holding as well in the fiberglass types of tree. I have always been very concerned about the safety issue when using synthetic trees.

The objects known as the "rigging rings" are sometimes round, sometimes dee shaped and are even made in odd forms that don't even resemble a ring. The usual materials are of iron, iron with chrome plating, stainless steel, aluminum, brass or bronze. The least desirable of these materials is iron, followed by chrome plated iron, because of its tendency to rust.

All riggings fall into three basic styles which are: *ring rigging, in-skirt* rigging and *flat plate* rigging.

The ring rigging is usually secured directly to the tree with the ring very close to the fork and this is a very strong style. The style is widely used in roping saddles. It has the advantage of great strength and the disadvantage of creating bulk under the rider's leg.

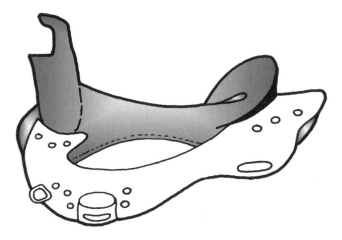

FLAT PLATE RIGGING

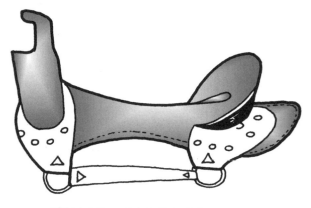

RING RIGGING

Because it is fastened close to the tree the ring riggings also restrict the forward swing of the stirrup leathers. When properly made they will allow considerable swing, but certainly not the freedom of flat-plate or in-skirt rigging.

There are some definite disadvantages to the ring rigging style. As I said, the stirrup leathers are hindered and don't swing as well. Because of the extra bulk caused by this style it becomes harder to feel the horse under your legs. Most ring rig saddles are made in the full position and on most horses the cinch will then be too far forward, which can create cinch sores. Because the ring rigging is so far forward, it allows the pivot action mentioned earlier, which makes the back of the saddle unstable.

When the tree is a pretty good fit to the horse's back a ring rigging in the full position isn't too bad, but if extra padding is required to make the tree fit properly this position will make the tree slide forward or back, and usually it's back. A saddle sliding backward will almost always cause sores on the shoulders and apply to much pressure to the kidney area. If the tree does fit, it can still move back when the rigging is set too far forward for the horse's conformation.

Most production saddles are made with ring rigging and have that rigging set in the full position. In fact,

probably 95 % of the saddles you see are ring rigged
or in-skirt rigged in the full position. The reason for
this is NOT because it is the best position, but only
because it is the easiest and cheapest position to use
when building a saddle. Production saddles are built
this way because, until now, how many riders knew
there was anything else? If they had heard of the other
methods, could they identify them, know what to ask
about them or even expect a knowledgeable answer
from the typical feed-store saddle salesman?!

<u>In-skirt</u> rigging is a term that indicates the ring, or plate,
is set into, and directly attached to, this saddle skirt
instead of rigging straps attached to the tree. This style
reduces bulk under the legs and gives a relatively free
swing to the stirrup leathers. In-skirt rigging is quite
popular with pleasure riders and is used widely by
barrel racers.

There are two basic styles of in-skirt rigging; *built-on*
and *built-in*. Built-on rigging is quite simply a plate
attached to the surface of the skirt. This is usually a
style used with inexpensive production saddles and is
not very strong or secure. Built-in riggings have a plate
on the surface of the skirt and are mostly covered with
more layers of leather which are sewn in tightly. This
plate is then riveted for security.

RIGGING IN-SKIRT STYLES

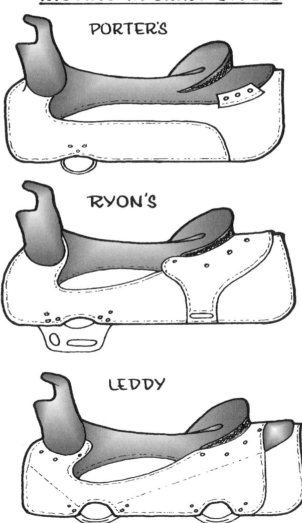

PORTER'S

RYON'S

LEDDY

Many well-known saddle shops have developed their own style of in-skirt riggings and the styles have been copied by the smaller shops. The styles used by Porter's, Ryon's and Leddy are most common. Each style has it's good points and it's bad points. I believe that in-skirt riggings have gotten a bad reputation because so many are used on poorly constructed, mass-produced saddles. When built correctly this rigging style can be very strong and will probably outlast the average ring rigging. It definitely takes more time, more leather and much greater skill than the average ring rigging and should, therefore, justify its greater expense. The only real drawback is that the skirts tend to cup and wrinkle around the plate and the plate itself can become deformed as the years go by and heavy use takes its toll.

The flat plate, in my opinion, is the king of all riggings. It is made similar to the in-skirt rigging, but is not attached to the skirts. It is made on a "plate" of leather. This plate usually consists of two or three layers of leather sewn together with a metal plate riveted securely to the point where the cinches attach. This plate is then solidly attached to the tree with a variety of screws and nails.

The chief advantages of the flat plate rigging are: superior strength, greater freedom of swing for the stirrup leathers, more uniform pull across the entire

FLATPLATE STYLES

RAY HOLE'S STYLE

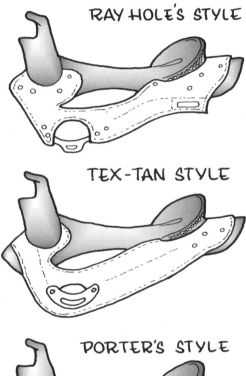

TEX-TAN STYLE

PORTER'S STYLE

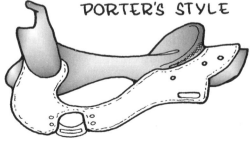

length of the tree and a lack of bulk under the knees which gives better contact with the horse. Because it is attached to the tree, and not to the skirts, it will never make the skirts bunch up or twist under pressure. (Also, the dee rings for attaching the breast collar should be in the plate and not in the skirts. This prevents a lot of twists and pressures on the skirts, too.) When made properly, the pressures applied when cinching a saddle with this type of rigging should pull approximately 60 percent on the front pads of the tree and 40 percent on the rear. I have found that a rear cinch is very rarely required when using this type of rigging, including light to medium roping chores.

Flat plate riggings are beginning to see a resurgence in popularity recently due to the growing concern for more properly built equipment. This style is seen in many of the saddles built from the 1930's through the early 1950's, at which time it almost disappeared. It surfaced again in the mid-70's and its popularity is growing fast. Just like in-skirt rigging, the flat plate has been made popular by a number of larger saddle shops and those styles have been copied and modified by custom makers. The only disadvantages that I have ever been able to find in the flat plate is slight additional bulk [one-half inch on each side of the saddle] and in the increased cost basis for the saddle. This type of rigging takes more time, materials and skill to make than the others. It is my strong opinion that this rigging is by far the safest and the best designed today and well worth the additional costs.

Regardless of the rigging position or style used, it is extremely important that the rigging be properly and perfectly aligned. The dees, rings or plates absolutely must be in exactly the same position from side to side. Slight differences in elevation may be acceptable, however, the distance from the front of the tree to the center of the plate or ring must be exact within one-quarter of an inch. This is a very difficult measurement to make on a finished saddle. The skilled, and conscientious saddlemaker checks this carefully when the rigging is installed. The reason this accuracy is so important is, for example, if the right side rigging was one inch further forward than the left rigging the entire saddle will twist to the right when the cinches are pulled tight. This will apply a great deal of pressure to the right front bar and the left rear bar point. In other words, the tree would be forced to "rock" on the horse's back. This rocking motion would not be very evident due to the softness of the saddle pad and the tissue making up the back, but it would eventually make itself known by sores being created as you ride. A great majority of the saddles that have been brought to me with the complaint that they make a horse sore have only needed to have the rigging reset correctly. There is no easy way for the average horseman to check this rigging accuracy, but I have seen some production saddles with the rigging rings as much as one and one-half inch out of alignment. This much alignment is visible to anyone who looks at it!

Also, a well built saddle has nails and screws to secure the riggings. Many production saddles use small rivets, tiny nails and, predominantly, staples. I consider saddles with staples to be extremely hazardous and fall in the class of "an accident looking for a place to happen".

Remember, the purpose of the rigging is to secure the tree to the horse in the most comfortable manner possible. It must be straight and correct. It must not interfere with the riders legs and it must allow as much forward and backward motion of the stirrup leathers as possible. As a general rule properly applied riggings will require that you use less pressure when cinching the horse. The skill and care required to construct this type of rigging are not likely to be found in most of the factory or production saddles available today.

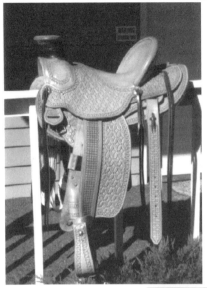

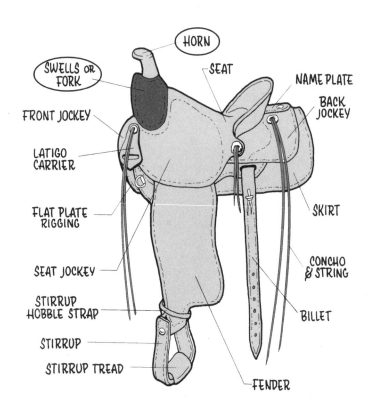

HORN

SWELLS OR FORK

SEAT

NAME PLATE

BACK JOCKEY

FRONT JOCKEY

LATIGO CARRIER

FLAT PLATE RIGGING

SEAT JOCKEY

STIRRUP HOBBLE STRAP

STIRRUP

STIRRUP TREAD

SKIRT

CONCHO & STRING

BILLET

FENDER

FORK COVER
and
HORNS

The *fork* is the strong, large piece attached to the front of the saddle near the end of the bars. The name given to the shape of the fork is the name that the entire tree carries without regard to the type of bars or cantle configuration. The horn is attached to the top center of this fork and has no bearing on the name of the tree.

In the old days the saddlemakers made this part of the saddle frame from the fork of a tree. In most cases the horn and the fork were cut from the same piece of wood. Some history books state that occasionally a strong fork of deer or elk antlers where was used, which led to the name "horn". Today most horns are made of steel or bronze. Remember, on a western saddle, this part is always referred to as the fork and never as the *pommel*!

The evolution of fork styles is very interesting to study. Many of the changes came about for specific working purposes and were created by working cowboys. There

89

are a great number of forks that have little basis in anything except popular style. There are as many different styles as there are riders and many of these riders have very logical explanations for their preference. On the other hand, many riders order strange fork styles just because they "look neat" and later realize that they are not very practical for their style of riding.

The two basic styles are *swell fork* and *smooth fork* (often referred to as the *slick fork* or *A-fork*). The original *A-fork* angled almost straight from the tree bars to the horn. This style, at the beginning, was very narrow and didn't offer much strength. The next step was to widen and thicken the A-fork and it became known as the "*narrow-fork*". This new style offered a greater strength while remaining close to the horse and out of the way for the serious roper. Next, in the evolution of the fork, came the extremely wide "ears" that some riders felt were needed for a better seat on a bronc. Some of the these wide forks grew from the 8 inch slick fork to the 24 inch, turned back, "freak" known as the "bear trap". This style of saddle made riding a bronc considerably easier but was almost impossible to get out of if the horse fell down. It was also regularly called a "widow maker".

As time went on these extra wide forks began to narrow until they reached more usable, and realistic,

FORKS

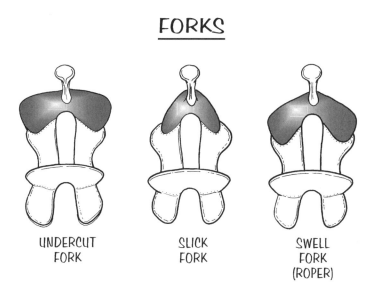

UNDERCUT   SLICK   SWELL
FORK   FORK   FORK
                                      (ROPER)

proportions. These became known as *swell forks*. To help define these styles draw an imaginary line from the outside attachment point of the fork straight up from the bar and if the fork does not extend beyond this point it is a *narrow fork*. Anything that extends beyond this is referred to as a *swell fork*.

Ropers prefer narrow swell saddles because the wider fork frequently catches the rope under the swell. Swell fork saddles are preferred for those who ride in rough country or who are riding more "resistant" horses because they give good support to brace the legs against and to help keep the rider in the saddle. Many riders, who prefer the A-fork style will fasten on a set of bucking rolls for the same purpose. These bucking rolls are then removed for normal riding. Today, however, I see bucking rolls as a permanent fixture on many saddles. I think these riders either don't understand the true function of the rolls or they are just trying to look like a "buckaroo".

Forks may be attached to the bars at various angles. The angle is judged from the hand hold to the top of the fork where the horn is attached. A very slight slope is considered *straight-up*. When the angle approaches approximately 15 to 20 degrees is called a *medium-slope*, and 25 to 40 degrees will be a *full slope*. The angle of the slope affects the space in the seat. A full slope, obviously, allows greater forward action in the seat. This would only be recommended for a very large rider. Cutting horse saddles are usually straight-up, while roping and pleasure saddles normally have a medium slope. Most A-fork saddles have a straight up slope, but it is difficult to see because the fork just seems to run into the ground seat. This is particularly true with the Wade style tree. The Wade is a very heavy slick fork style which is popular with the ranch ropers. At the time of this writing there is a strong resurgence in A-fork rigs owing to both practicality and nostalgia. Popular styles are the Weatherly, Old Style Visalia, F.L.Roper and the 3-B Visalia.

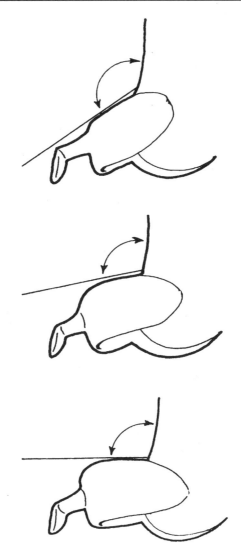

FORKS SHOWING DIFFERENT SLOPES

FULL SLOPE

MEDIUM SLOPE

STRAIGHT UP

MEASURING THE GULLET

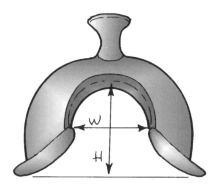

While evaluating the fork, always be mindful of the gullet. The gullet should have sufficient height to clear the horse's withers [without a pad] and enough width to sit comfortably behind the shoulders. If the gullet is too wide, the bars will sit too far down on the horse's sides and will make the bottom of the fork rub on top of the withers. If the horse has unusually high withers proper padding can help, but will not cure a poor fitting saddle. When sitting improperly the bars will also dig into places that will cause problems in a short period of time. (refer back to the chapter on TREES) Remember the old rule of "two fingers clearance between the gullet and the withers". Any shorter than that will definitely injure the horse.

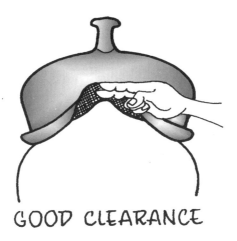

GOOD CLEARANCE

Forks may be covered with either leather or rawhide. White rawhide has been a popular fork cover in recent years and is very durable, however, it is a quick and cheap way to apply a cover and will not allow attractive decoration. It is most commonly seen on manufactured saddles.

Higher quality saddles have good skirting leather fork covers which are usually decorated with carving, stamping, stitching or a combination of these elements.

The front edge of the fork may be treated in a number of ways. The leather can be turned under and into the gullet, scallop cut and fastened with brass escutcheon pins. It can also have a *welt roll* by having the front

FORK COVER STYLES

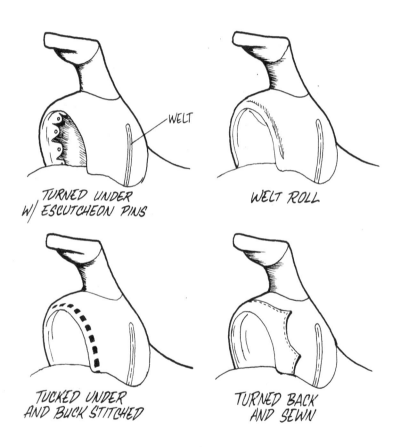

WELT

TURNED UNDER
W/ ESCUTCHEON PINS

WELT ROLL

TUCKED UNDER
AND BUCK STITCHED

TURNED BACK
AND SEWN

edge turned under and stretched into place. This can be accomplished by gluing it underneath, by being tucked under and stitched or by been tucked under and buck stitched. A very decorative style seen fairly often is a scalloped piece of leather, or rawhide, placed under the fork cover, turned back and sewn.

If the saddle has *undercut swells* it is necessary to remove excess leather from the fork cover. This is accomplished with the use of a *welt seam*. The welt fills the cut created by removing this extra leather. If the leather was just sewn together and stretched over the fork the stitching would show and would be susceptible to damage. With the welt the stitching is hidden and well protected. On high quality saddles the welt will be made of a folded piece of leather inserted into the seam. Working saddles usually have a single piece of leather in this seam which is finished quite nicely.

Another method of closing the seam is the *laced welt*. Sometimes this is accomplished with a single strand of leather and can be very attractive. Occasionally, a saddlemaker will use multiple strands of lace and create a very pretty braid over the seam. Although these are very nice to look at they don't wear well and will probably require repair or replacement in a short time.

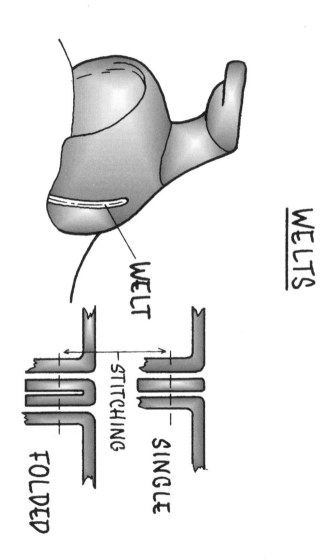

WELTS

WELT

STITCHING

FOLDED

SINGLE

Production saddles often use a *butt seam* instead of a welt. The edges of the leather are butted together and stitched from the back side at an angle through half the thickness of the leather. This is a very inferior construction technique and will not stand hard use. It is also very difficult to repair.

The angle of the seam is of little importance. It can be a straight line from the point of the fork to the bar; it can be from the point forward towards the gullet; or it can be back towards the seat and still accomplish the same task. Its position is only one of style and convenience for the maker.

Another part sometimes found on the fork is the *rope strap*. The strap is usually made of a piece of leather, approximately 3/4 inch wide and attached to the off [right] side of the fork. Its purpose is to hold the lariat. Most working riders prefer a slot cut in the end of this strap which makes a loop to go over the horn. If the rider becomes entangled in the rope, this loop will break and, hopefully, prevent a terrible accident.

HORNS

Horns come in as many shapes and styles as one can imagine. Horn styles, like much of the saddle, are dictated by their use and by current fashion. Most saddle horns are made of bronze or steel. When they're made of metal they usually have four legs which are countersunk and bolted into the fork before the rawhide is applied. The bolts and rawhide make the horn a very solid part of the tree.

INSTALLING THE HORN

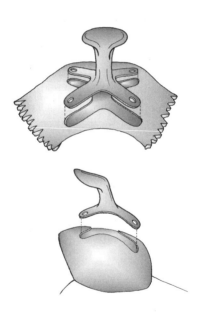

In the old days horns were made of bronze or nickel and were highly polished and left exposed. However, the steel horn is stronger and more adaptable but it has a tendency to rust. As a result, the steel horn is always covered with leather or rawhide. The wood-post horn is usually carved from the same piece of wood as the fork and has no metal in it, unless it is carved separately and attached with lag bolts [definitely not the highest quality].

HOW TO MEASURE A HORN

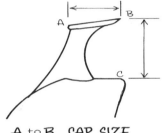

A to B   CAP SIZE
B to C   HORN HEIGHT

Horn measurements are taken from the base straight up to the edge of the top for the height and from edge to edge on the top for the cap size.

The treemaker can set the horn at any desired angle on top of the fork. The style of roping and the purpose of the saddle dictate the position and angle of the horn.

HORN SLOPES

FORWARD   MEDIUM   STRAIGHT

Horns can be chosen in such a variety of neck lengths, neck diameters, cap sizes and head pitch (angle) that I could fill an entire book with photos and measurements. Let me just say that if you are ordering a custom saddle, choose the horn carefully to suit your needs. Also please remember that you see this part of the saddle most of the time so it must be pleasing to your eye. This is something that you have no control over when you are buying a ready made or a used saddle. It can be changed, but it will never be as strong as it should be.

The *horn cap*, on lesser grade saddles, is made of two pieces of leather which are sewn together. High grade saddles will use three pieces of leather in the horn cap; the center piece (sometimes called the *filler*) is usually tacked to the top of the horn to prevent it from ever becoming loose and wiggly. Some horn caps are made with a leather or rawhide binding over the edge. The rawhide binding makes them particularly durable for hard work, but it is an expensive option as rawhide is more difficult to work with.

If the saddle is to be used for roping, a horn wrap should be applied. This is a piece of leather that is wrapped tightly around the horns neck which increases the diameter and absorbs some of the abrasion of the rope. This neck wrap is also a good idea for pleasure saddles because it will protect the neck from the abrasion of hanging binoculars, canteens, purses, halters and other "necessary" items.

The two most common materials used for horn wraps are *latigo leather* and *"mule hide"*. Mulehide does not come from mules but is a heavy gray split leather used for farrier chaps and welding aprons. It is widely used for horn wraps, but no one is quite sure how it got the name mulehide. I guess it's just because it sounds better than "apron leather". I prefer the look of burgundy colored latigo because it looks more finished and doesn't soil as easily.

Sometimes the horn neck is wrapped with a piece of inner tube cut like an oversized rubber band. This serves to help the dally roper control the speed that his roping is playing out around the horn and gives him greater stopping power when applying pressure to the rope.

A man once told me that the creation of ropers and roping was really God's little joke on mankind and He did it just to show He had a wonderful sense of humor .... God began by gathering up all of the necessary elements: a large, four footed bovine creature with relatively little intelligence that weighs about 1600 pounds; next on the list is a large, four footed equine creature that weighs about 1200 pounds, also with relatively limited intelligence; then He added to this

group a two footed humanoid creature that weighs
about 160 pounds, with questionable intelligence.
Finally, just for fun, He tied all three together with an
unbreakable nylon cord! ----This has created an
unlimited variety of disastrous and humorous events
which continue to amuse Him to this day.

"...just for fun, He tied all three together with an unbreakable nylon cord!"

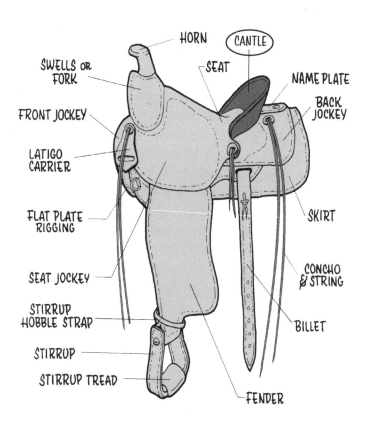

HORN
CANTLE
SEAT
SWELLS or FORK
NAME PLATE
FRONT JOCKEY
BACK JOCKEY
LATIGO CARRIER
FLAT PLATE RIGGING
SKIRT
SEAT JOCKEY
CONCHO & STRING
STIRRUP HOBBLE STRAP
STIRRUP
BILLET
STIRRUP TREAD
FENDER

CANTLES

The *cantle* is the back of the seat and prevents the rider from sliding off the back end of the horse. It also gives the rider a comfortable support to lean against whether the horse is moving or standing.

The cantle has gone through a great series of evolution just as the fork did. It was very low for early military saddles and extremely high-backed in the medieval times when the mounted knight used it to support his lance. Eventually the cantle worked its way down to about 4 inches and has undergone relatively little change since 1700. In the days of the American frontier, and the long the cattle drives, the cantle again increased in height up to the six inch "high back cantle". Those drovers needed comfort and security.

In the 1950's and 1960's, very low cantles became popular. These were as low as 2" and were of little use or function. Happily, they have fallen out of favor in recent years.

CANTLE SHAPES

REGULAR

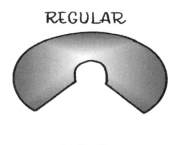

COMFORT

SHOVEL

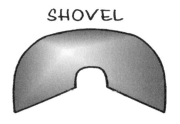

Cantles come in the three basic shapes of *regular, comfort* and *shovel* as I discussed in the earlier chapter about trees. The cantle height is measured at the back side from the bars to the top and the width is measured straight across the front from the widest point on each side. The normal width is about 12 inches and the "average" height is three to four inches. This height can vary a great deal in accordance with the rider's wishes.

The cantle slope or pitch may also vary according to the rider's wishes and the purpose for which he will use his rig.

All good saddles have a *binding* which covers the top edge. This binding may be made of leather or rawhide. (Rawhide is more durable and, also, more expensive because it is harder for the saddlemaker to work with.)

CANTLE SLOPE OR PITCH

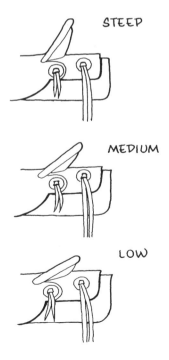

STEEP

MEDIUM

LOW

The reason for the binding is to hold together the leather from the back of the cantle and from the front, which is part of the seat. This also gives a very nice finished appearance to the entire saddle. Typically, production saddles have this binding sewn by machine to both pieces of leather before this assembly is placed on the saddle tree. It is stretched, and sometimes glued, over the cantle. After a short period of time this cantle binding will become soft and it can be moved back and forth easily.

A well made saddle has a cantle binding which is sewn by hand. The biggest difference, which makes for a firmer and more durable binding, is the addition of a *filler*. This filler is a another piece of leather which is sometimes nailed to the cantle and sometimes is an extension of the final ground seat piece. The purpose of this filler is to stiffen the binding and to secure the entire assembly to the tree so that it will never loosen or become soft.

The binding leather is folded over the cantle front, the filler and the cantle back. This creates a thickness of five pieces of leather. Because of the positioning on the edge of the cantle there is no way to stitch this, in place, with a machine. The saddlemaker must sew it by hand and usually does this with a hand held awl, two needles and waxed cord. This is very difficult

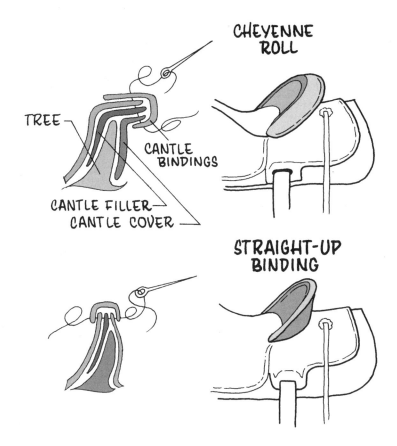

CHEYENNE ROLL

TREE

CANTLE BINDINGS

CANTLE FILLER
CANTLE COVER

STRAIGHT-UP BINDING

and perfectly uniform stitches show the hand of an accomplished craftsman. Some saddlemakers use a method called "the hidden stitch". To do this they carefully split the binding on the back side, complete their stitching and then glue this split leather back down over the stitches. This can be a difficult method, but it is very attractive and shows a concern for quality.

The *Cheyenne roll* is very popular and is seen on most production saddles today. Tradition tells us that this style cantle binding was first made in the Cheyenne, Wyoming, saddle Shop of Frank Meanea. It is a flat shelf of leather that is folded back at a 90 degree angle from the top of the cantle. It also contains a filler, the cantle back leather and the cantle front leather (part of the seat). When this is machine stitched and then slipped into place it is very thin and lacks firmness. A soft and flimsy Cheyenne roll is one of the first signs of a cheap saddle. No particular purpose for the roll has ever been discovered and it should be considered mostly ornamental. I have heard some say that the Cheyenne roll "softened" the blow when they were thrown out of the saddle and landed back down on the cantle. I find this hard to believe because the Cheyenne roll tilts slightly down from the edge of the cantle leaving the hard edge still available to land on. I have heard others say that it was there to hold on to when their horse became "broncy". I find this even harder to believe. If the horse is going to buck why would a rider want to twist a shoulder and his torso to the back in order to grab the roll and, in so doing, throw off his balance and center of gravity? I do find the Cheyenne roll to be a very convenient hand-hold when throwing a saddle up on the horse's back, but not much other purpose can be discovered.

I am often asked my opinion of the perfect height for a cantle. I believe that most working saddles, and pleasure saddles, are best with a four inch cantle. This gives sufficient back support and security for most situations. A person who plans to spend long hours in the saddle might prefer a five to six inch cantle to get even more support. I have heard many ropers tell me that anything over three inches slows them down. Videos have proven that when they get off their leg clears a four inch cantle with lots of room to spare and that height is not a factor. The videos have also shown that the taller cantle holds the ropers in place better and improves his riding. Now when the horse comes out of the roping box that cowboy is not fighting to stay in the saddle but is held firmly in place and can concentrate on his rope instead of his riding.

Remember when looking at the cantle that the key item is comfort and durability, with style coming in way back in third place!

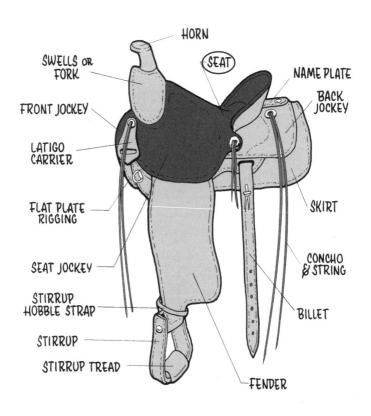

HORN

SWELLS OR
FORK

SEAT

NAME PLATE

BACK
JOCKEY

FRONT JOCKEY

LATIGO
CARRIER

FLAT PLATE
RIGGING

SKIRT

SEAT JOCKEY

CONCHO
& STRING

STIRRUP
HOBBLE STRAP

BILLET

STIRRUP

STIRRUP TREAD

FENDER

SEATS

The saddle *seat*, like everything else connected with the saddle, has been subject to a lot of changes. In the early days the *three-quarter seat* saddle was most common in the West. This type of rig had a leather seat that stopped just short of the stirrup leathers. The jockeys were not usually a part of the seat, either. It was not comfortable primarily because there was not enough space to properly shape a ground seat. The lack of jockeys with this style of saddle also was distressful because the stirrup leathers often pinched the rider's thighs. This style was quite prevalent from about 1870 through the early 1900's.

Next came the *loop seat*. A single, large piece of leather covered the entire seat and jockey area and extended upward to the fork by the handhold. A rectangular opening was cut out of the seat over the positon where each of the stirrup leathers went over the bars. This made it easy to examine, clean and change them. With

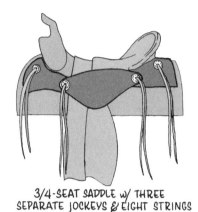

3/4-SEAT SADDLE w/ THREE
SEPARATE JOCKEYS & EIGHT STRINGS

this style seat the front jockeys were usually made separately from the rest of the seat and a concho with string was positioned at the base of the fork to hold the pieces together. This style is known as the *eight-string style*. Over the years the loop seat proved to be undesirable because the openings also made it easy for water and dirt to enter the saddle and deteriorate the condition of the seat leather and stirrup leathers.

Finally we arrived at the *full seat*. A single piece of leather covering the cantle, side jockeys, seat and front jockeys. With this improvement the number 2 concho and saddle string at the base of the fork was replaced with a small screw. This created the *six-string style*.

The primary criteria for a long lasting saddle is a comfortable seat. The important elements are the slope, angle, width, and sufficient seat and leg space. If these items are the wrong size or constructed improperly the rider can experience backaches, leg pain, hip discomfort and, even headaches.

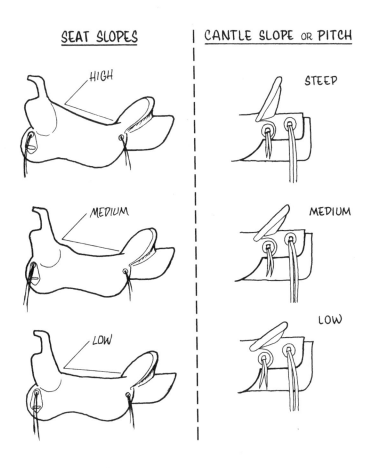

SEAT SLOPES | CANTLE SLOPE OR PITCH

HIGH

MEDIUM

LOW

STEEP

MEDIUM

LOW

Many combinations of these angles are possible

Another factor that affects seat size is the amount of
slope of the fork. A wide fork that is straight up will
certainly crowd a rider more than the same fork with a
full forward slope. With the A-fork styles this is not
very important as there is always sufficient leg room
and a well made slick-fork saddle always has a natural
position for the thighs to fit.

FORKS SHOWING DIFFERENT SLOPES

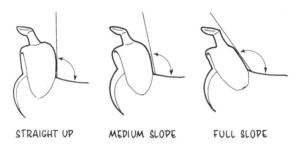

STRAIGHT UP   MEDIUM SLOPE   FULL SLOPE

If the saddle seat is uncomfortable the rider will
unconsciously move about trying to find a "home".
This continual movement will cause uneven weight
distribution on the horse's back and can be a leading
cause of saddle sores.

To illustrate this, I imagine carrying my small daughter
in a backpack carrier. When she is asleep her weight
is easy to adjust to I can trudge down the path, but
when she awakens she leans to the left to view a

butterfly, leans to the right to see a chipmonk, and so forth. This moves the weight distribution all over my back and, as a result, I become uncomfortable. I then change the position of my backbone and the muscles that support the backpack. Voila!! Back sores!! This is exactly what happens on a horse's back when the rider is unable to maintain a regular position in the saddle. After all, isn't the tree just another form of backpack frame?

All of this shows just how important a good seat is. The basis of this seat is the ground work under the seat cover. Refer back to the chapter about *Ground Seats* for more details. Always consider the seat size first, as measured from the base of the horn to the top of the cantle. The actual sitting area is then controlled by the amount of slope in the base of the seat and the slope of the cantle. Study the illustrations and you will easily understand the relationship between these two angles.

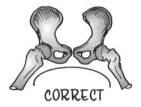

CORRECT

TOO ROUND

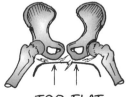

TOO FLAT

The most important factor is the area that the pelvic bones rest upon. Too flat and you ride on the point of the bones; too round and you force the bones apart and ride on the tailbone!

Many saddles today have a pad to help make them comfortable. Pads have been around for many years. In the early 1900's the saddles made for ladies were either *side-saddles* or *astride-saddles*. Most of the side saddles had a heavy piece of carpeting on their seat. The astride saddles had extremely heavy padding which looked more like quilting. (By the way, early padding was stuffed with sheepskin, cotton, cloth and, even, grass!)

Contrary to popular opinion, a "soft" seat is not comfortable, it merely allows for any pressure points to go unnoticed longer before "butt fatigue" sets in. Soft seats also allow excessive pressure at unwanted points such as the sensitive nerves in the lower pelvic area. I have found that the "hard seat" (i.e. NO padding) when correctly contoured is more comfortable all day long, day after day. Don't look for softness. Look instead for a firm equalization of pressure for extended comfort for both you and the horse.

Another drawback to the padded seat is its ability to collect water! If it is made of open-cell foam material it will absorb and hold water. Water from rain, snow and, on hot days, sweat. If it is made of closed-cell foam it will not absorb water, but it will also not breathe and will cause more heat on your own sitting parts than is desirable. Either way, it can be an uncomfortable ride over a period of time.

Any pad material used must have a cover and that cover must be thin in order to flex with the softness underneath. With this thinner material being exposed to the most constant abrasion it is bound to wear out first and require repair while the rest of the saddle is still in good shape. A custom saddle should last a long time without repairs! Also, if you decide you must have a padded seat you should add one inch to the seat length to allow for the space the padding will take up.

With all of the above information I am sure you are asking "why are there padded seats, anyway?". The reasons are many: they look good; they make you think the saddle fits better; they cover cheaply made saddles! Many manufactured saddles have seats made of two pieces of leather. These are made by companies that are not interested in doing the work or spending the time necessary to carefully stretch, cut and fit a seat tightly into the cantle area and over the seat (a difficult chore, at best!). These manufactured saddles have padded seats to cover the seam where the parts are joined together.

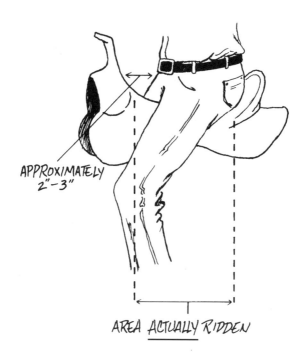

APPROXIMATELY
2"-3"

AREA ACTUALLY RIDDEN

Usually a pad covers an inferior seat, but some high quality saddles still have pads due to customer requests. These would be sewn directly onto a properly constructed seat and only enhance a comfortable rig. This type of pad is usually evident due to being very thin and not having much "give" when pushed.

An experienced saddlemaker will build the type of seat that matches your riding style: low or almost flat seats for today's cutting horses; deep seats for roping and ranch horses; equitation seats for show horses. These are not "rules", only generalities. All types of seats can be found in pleasure saddles.

The most important thing is that the saddle fits you.

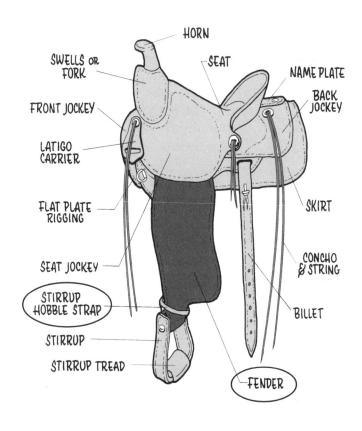

HORN

SWELLS OR FORK

SEAT

NAME PLATE

FRONT JOCKEY

BACK JOCKEY

LATIGO CARRIER

FLAT PLATE RIGGING

SKIRT

SEAT JOCKEY

CONCHO & STRING

STIRRUP HOBBLE STRAP

BILLET

STIRRUP

STIRRUP TREAD

FENDER

STIRRUP LEATHERS
and
FENDERS

The *stirrup leathers* are the long, wide straps that attach the stirrups to the saddle tree. The stirrup leathers can be any size ranging from the heavy one inch strap used on English saddles to the three inch wide straps used on most Western saddles. With some barrel racing and pleasure saddles two inch or two and one-half inch straps are common. This narrow size can be a cost cutting method and these straps are often found on the cheaper factory-made saddles.

Since a broken stirrup strap can cause a rider to lose his balance and be thrown from the horse, top quality leather must always be used. I believe that the quality of the stirrup leathers is one of the most important safety factors in the making of a saddle. The stirrup leathers should always be cut from the same cowhide and from the same direction on that hide. This will help ensure that, over time, the stirrup leathers will stretch the same. A top saddlemaker usually pre-stretches the stirrup leathers before putting them together.

125

MODERN
FENDER

OLD STYLE
FENDER

The amount of stretch and the precise location of the adjustment holes in the stirrup leathers are very important. Should the stirrup leathers stretch differently one side will become longer than the other. When the rider applies weight to the stirrups the saddle will begin to twist to the side that has the shorter stirrup. This will place an uneven stress on the horse's back, will tend to make the saddle blankets move and will, eventually, create discomfort and back sores. Many saddles that have been brought to me for repair because they caused saddle sores only needed the stirrup leathers restretched or the holes punched more uniformly for the quick change buckles. Sometimes the problem was as simple as the rider not counting the same number of holes on either side.

A great deal is said about "free swinging" stirrups. I think free swinging stirrups are grossly over-rated. There have been many devices made to create free swinging stirrups; metal pivoting hangers riveted to the tree, metal bars secured to the bottom of the tree bars, and even slots cut into the tree bars themselves. Along with many other things that are wrong with these methods they also weaken the tree.

How much free swinging do we really need? When sitting in the saddle our legs can only extend forward at a maximum 50 degree angle. Any greater angle causes a loss of contact with the horse and a loss of balance. Rear swing never exceeds 20 degrees. More swing than this is excessive and, perhaps, dangerous. Dangerous because it wouldn't allow the rider to apply the pressures needed to maintain a solid seat.

The stirrup leathers should hang over the tree bars and extend downward beneath the seat jockeys. To achieve maximum swing there must be adequate clearance under the ground seat. The stirrup leathers must also be able to swing forward without coming in contact with the rigging straps. This is the chief advantage to the flat-plate rigging. When properly made a flat-plate is trimmed near the top so that the stirrup leathers do not come in contact with it, while the ring rigging must be fastened below the edges of the fork where the leathers will bump into them at 30 degrees or less.

Stirrup leathers should be hung from the tree in a position that is just behind the rider's knees. In an attempt to make saddles feel as though they have more "free swing" some outfits are made today with the stirrup leathers hung much further forward. With this kind of a setup when pressure is applied to the stirrups it forces the rider back and tighter into the cantle. If that rider were to stand in the stirrups he would be standing over the fork and horn. Stirrup leathers that are hung too far forward will create excessive pressure on the horse's shoulders and work against weight distribution over the length of the tree.

I have had some riders express a desire to have the stirrup leathers set farther back and almost straight down from their center of gravity. This, also, would be unsafe and very uncomfortable. Stirrup leathers must be hung somewhat forward to fit the human anatomy. Prove this to yourself by sitting on a tall stool. Where are your legs? Drop your legs straight down on either side of the stool and try to push forward or back. Notice how your balance and center of gravity is changed? Now, consider this same action while on the horse and it will be easy to understand why stirrup leathers set too far back can be dangerous.

As I stated earlier, stirrup leathers should be full length from the buckles onward. Some saddlemakers, and most factories, attach short cut stirrup leathers to the top and bottom of the fenders. Sometimes these are laced, sewn, riveted or a combination of these methods. When constructed this way the fender takes the place of the center of the stirrup strap. The fender then must bear all the stress and strain of any weight applied to the stirrups. The fender leather, being wider and cut from another area of the cowhide, is sure to stretch differently and will cause the stirrups to become uneven. The attachment method used at the top of the fender is also suspect and could be the cause of a accident. The only advantage to the half-style stirrup straps is limited width. They are very narrow, having

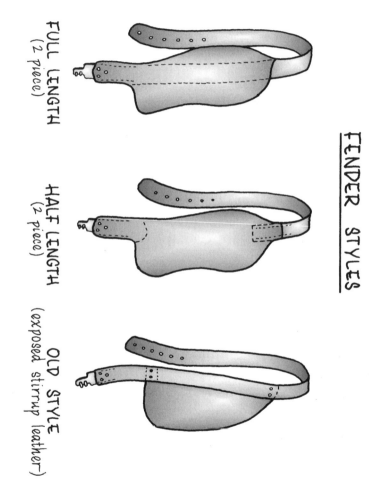

FULL LENGTH
(2 piece)

HALF LENGTH
(2 piece)

OLD STYLE
(exposed stirrup leather)

FENDER STYLES

one layer of leather removed from each side. This only makes the saddle one half inch closer to the horse (under the legs, not under the thighs) and doesn't seem worth the risks that go along with this lack of strength.

The *fenders* prevent the horse's sweat from getting on the rider. They're also known as *sweat leathers*. Fenders are made in a wide variety of shapes and sizes. In the modern styles the stirrup strap is hidden, or behind, the fender and it is cut with a bit of a forward sweep to prevent the rider's leg from making contact with the horse.

The style of the fender should correspond to the style of the saddle. In other words, if the saddle has old time square skirts it doesn't look right to have fenders which are curved to compliment a round skirt saddle. The shape at the top is very important. It must taper up to the stirrup leather and not be too wide under the seat jockey. This narrow trim makes for less bulk under the jockeys and allows the stirrup leathers their full swing. At the bottom the stirrup should hang down approximatley four inches and should never be tight up to the bottom of the fender. Again, this is so there is enough room for freedom of action where the stirrup swivels.

Stirrup leathers must have some means of a length adjustment. The old method of merely lacing the straps

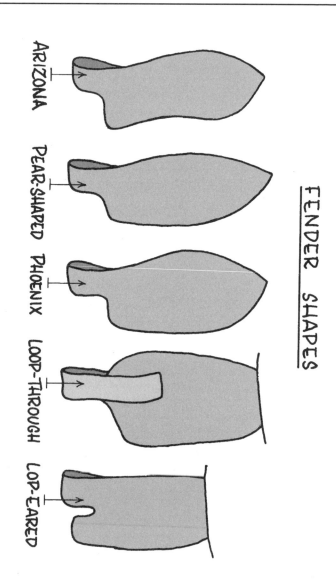

ARIZONA

PEAR-SHAPED

PHOENIX

LOOP-THROUGH

LOP-EARED

FENDER SHAPES

together with strong leather thongs was very practical
for the working cowboy who needed to do a quick
repair in the field. Changing the stirrup-strap length
for various riders of the same saddle made this method,
which was very slow, impractical for general use.
Quick change buckles have come into common use in
recent years to address this problem.

There are many types of the *quick change buckles*
available today. The best of these, and the easiest to
use, is the Blevins New Improved buckle. This style
has a leather covered sleeve and two pegs which insert
into pre-punched holes. Adjustments are quick and
easy. Most saddlemakers use ten to twelve holes with
this type of buckle which allows a very wide range of
stirrup strap lengths.

More important than the type of adjuster used is the
installation. The buckle should be about 10 to 14
inches from the lowest wide point of the fender. After
bending around the stirrup swivel, this distance will
put the buckle midway between the rider's ankle and
knee. If they are higher than this they will cause great
bulk under the knee and will rub the horse. If they are
too low they will interfer with the twist (or set) of the
stirrup and will rub the rider.

Another very important part of this fender/stirrup strap arrangement are the *hobble straps*. The hobble straps are placed around the outside of the fender extension and the stirrup straps and are just above the stirrups themselves.

STIRRUP HOBBLE

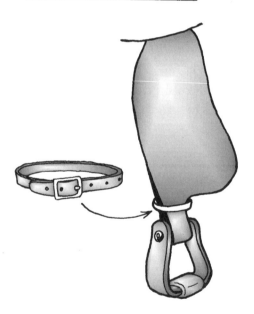

Their primary purpose is to close this "loop" and prevent the stirrups from turning over sideways and trapping a rider's foot. This is a safety measure that is very important. So important, in fact, that I would never consider allowing a child to ride any saddle without proper hobble straps installed!

The secondary function of the hobble straps is to help maintain the *set*, or turn, in the stirrup leathers. Most new saddles have the stirrups hang parallel with the fenders. This makes finding the off-side stirrup difficult when mounting and creates pressure on the knees while attempting to hold the foot in proper position. All saddles should have the stirrups set at 90 degrees to the fender, in order that the foot goes into a natural position when riding. All top quality saddlemakers build this into their saddles before final construction.

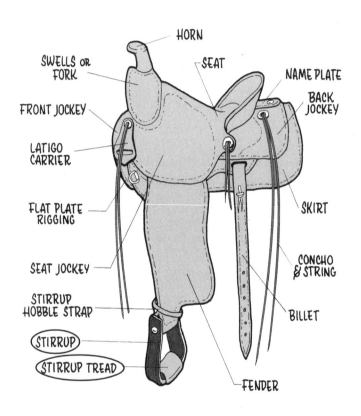

HORN

SWELLS or FORK

SEAT

NAME PLATE

FRONT JOCKEY

BACK JOCKEY

LATIGO CARRIER

FLAT PLATE RIGGING

SKIRT

SEAT JOCKEY

CONCHO & STRING

STIRRUP HOBBLE STRAP

BILLET

STIRRUP

STIRRUP TREAD

FENDER

STIRRUPS

The *stirrup* is the open loop at the bottom of the fender into which you put your foot. That sounds pretty simple and you would think that saddles always had a place for your feet. However, that is not the case. Historians tell us that mankind rode horses for hundreds, perhaps thousands, of years with only a pad and surcingle before the invention of the saddle and had nothing to put their feet into for stability and security. Historians also considered the invention of the stirrups to be the most significant military advance until the invention of gun powder many centuries later. Having some kind of stirrup gave the horse-soldier the necessary stability to do combat while mounted horseback. Again, referring to the historians, we're told that for the first few hundred years the stirrup used was only a small.ring attached to the strap fastened to the surcingle. This ring was about two inches in diameter, was probably made of wood or bone and, later, could have been created in bronze metal.

The interesting thing is that the rider only inserted his
<u>big toe!</u>

While the origin of stirrups remains clouded in history
it is likely, however that soft
strap-like stirrups existed
probably among the
nomadic horsemen of Asia.
As time passed, and stirrup
designs evolved, their use
spread across the known
world. Eventually the
stirrup reached Spain and
the carved stirrup evolved.

EARLY SPANISH
(HANDCARVED WOOD)

Still later saddlemakers began making stirrups of many types of wood. This wood was steam heated and bent into the desired shape. It was then covered (much later in history) with galvanized sheet metal to increase its strength.

The next improvement was to cover the entire stirrup with leather and to add a tread to reduce wear and extend the useful life of the stirrup.

The stirrup has six parts, each of which is very important to its function and its overall safety. The *tread* reduces wear, the *galvanized covers* increase strength, the *roller pipe* allows freedom of movement and the *bolt wear leather* prevents wear and discoloration to the stirrup leathers.

BOLT WEAR LEATHER

BOLT

SIDEPIECES
(GALVANIZED IRON)

ROLLER
(UNDER WEAR-LEATHER)

TREAD

TREAD WEAR LEATHER

SIDE VIEW

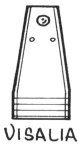

VISALIA

MORAN

BELL BOTTOM

The name of the stirrup is derived from its profile shape. *Visalia* is evenly tapered from the base to the roller; the *Moran* has a more graceful curve to the sides; and the *Bell Bottom* is very wide in the tread area. These are known as box stirrups.

The shape of a stirrup also is named. the most common being the Roper, Oxbow, Overshoe and Bronc.

The Roper is the most common and is used for a wide variety of saddles. The Oxbow is usually seen on old-timer style saddles and is more common in the northwestern states. The Overshoe is larger than the others and is truly intended for use with overshoes or mud-boots. The bronc stirrup is rarely seen outside of the rodeo arena as it is not very comfortable for long riding.

FRONT VIEW

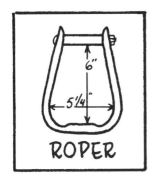

ROPER

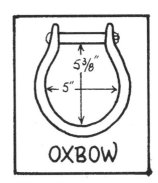

OXBOW

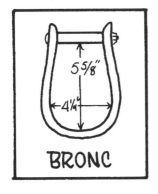

BRONC

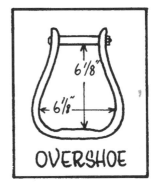

OVERSHOE

Saddlemakers can order custom stirrups to fit any need. The proper way to measure a stirrup is on the inside for height and width. The roller pipe should always be 3 1/8" to fit the standard 3" stirrup leather. In the case of some ladies' saddles or youth saddles this might be brought down to 2 5/8".

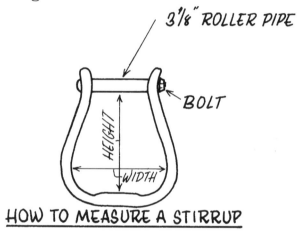

HOW TO MEASURE A STIRRUP

A later development in stirrup covers was the *tapadero* (or *tap*) which was widely used in the Southwest. This was designed to protect the rider's boots from the mesquite and heavy brush. Taps also keep the feet somewhat warmer in northern climates. They can be very helpful in preventing the foot from getting caught in the stirrup, particularly on children's saddles.

TAPADEROS

MONKEY NOSE

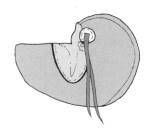

MONKEY FACE

SHIELD

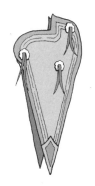

EAGLE BILL

Like all other saddle parts, the tap was subject to ornamentations and eventually became lengthened to extend well below the stirrup to add to the appearance of the saddle and the rider. While most taps do not extend longer than 8" to 12" below the stirrup, occassionaly they are seen to be as much as 28" long! At this length they start to add considerable weight and might affect the rider's balance at times.

Cheaper saddles have unbound stirrups with only a lightweight tread. Today it is common to find plastic or fiberglass stirrups on these cheap rigs. Some even have leather carving designs cast into their sides!

Iron, bronze and aluminum stirrups have become popular over the years. These can be very attractive, but many riders find them to be excessively cold in bad weather. Heavy stirrups can be an advantage in that they stay in place and are easily found when mounting in a hurry. On the other hand, they can be a real hazard if you are hit by one of them.

The Oxbow stirrup requires a slightly different riding style. The foot is pushed in all the way to the heel of the boot. This also requires a good steel arch in the boots to distribute the weight across the foot. This style is very old and is frequently made of iron or brass. Metal stirrups require a leather tread to prevent cold from working up through the boots.

PROPER FOOT POSITION
FOR OXBOW STIRRUP

PROPER FOOT POSITION
FOR BELL BOTTOM STIRRUP

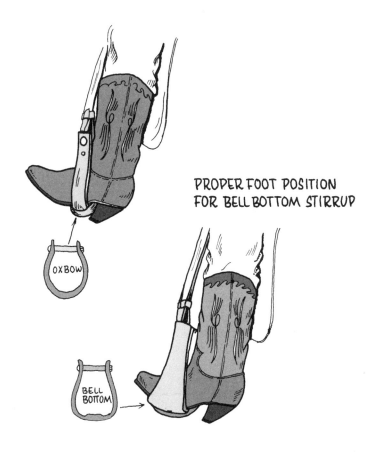

OXBOW

BELL
BOTTOM

By comparison, the box stirrup is wide and flat across the base which allows the rider to use the entire sole of the boot to give support to the front of the foot. With this style the heel is never in contact with the stirrup and the heel is down. All other styles of stirrups (with the only exception being the Oxbow) are ridden this way. These riding styles are purely personal preference and there is no right stirrup or style!

Good horsemanship requires proper positioning of the stirrup to ensure proper seat position. A good rule of thumb is that when you drop your foot from the stirrup the anklebone should strike the stirrup tread. This should lift you approximately 3" from the saddle when you stand in the stirrups. Too short a stirrup length probably feels more secure, but it forces the legs too far forward and too long a stirrup causes the legs to drop back. Neither of these positions will allow a rider to maintain a good center of balance.

For safety sake, always check the stirrup length and be sure the buckles are secure before each ride. Also, be sure to check that the saddle remains square over your horse's backbone during a ride. Remember, if the stirrups lengths are different the saddle will be pulled over to the side with the most pressure (short stirrup) and may cause saddle sores. Because most people have one leg slightly shorter than the other this is an easily overlooked cause of uneven weight distribution.

Another important factor to check is the condition of the stirrup. I have found many covered stirrups to be broken inside and the owners were unaware of it. Try to twist and flex the stirrup. If it moves replace it immediately! A broken stirrup can cause a wreck as quickly as anything and it is a serious safety hazard.

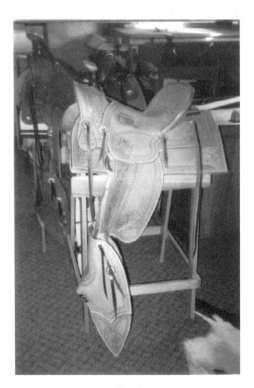

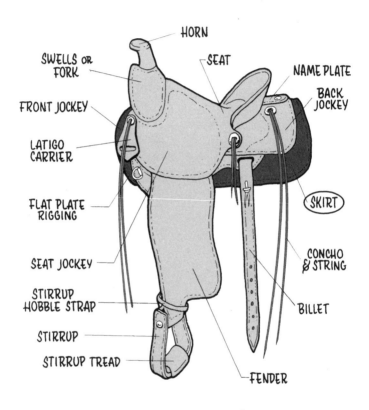

HORN

SWELLS OR
FORK

SEAT

NAME PLATE

BACK
JOCKEY

FRONT JOCKEY

LATIGO
CARRIER

FLAT PLATE
RIGGING

SKIRT

SEAT JOCKEY

CONCHO
& STRING

STIRRUP
HOBBLE STRAP

BILLET

STIRRUP

STIRRUP TREAD

FENDER

SKIRTS

Skirts are the large pieces of leather underneath the bars of the saddle tree. Originally the complete skirt was made from one large piece of leather. All skirts today are made in two pieces and laced or sewn together at the back. This is because it is less expensive to use two pieces of leather and because using two pieces creates an air channel the full length of the backbone which helps to cool the horse's back. The purpose of the skirts is to distribute the rider's weight and to protect the horse's back from the bars. Without the skirts the bars would sit directly on the horse's back separated only by the saddle pad. This would decrease the weight-per-square inch ratio and would add a greater amount of stress to the back.

Saddles, such as the Western stock saddle, which are intended to be used for working stock or being ridden for long hours at a time usually have skirts to help distribute weight and to keep sweat off the rider. This is evident when looking at saddles around the world;

149

Mexican charro saddles, South American Stock saddles, Afghanistan saddles, saddles from the Steppes of Asia, etc. and other non-sporting saddles.

Saddle skirts are made in two basic shapes, *square* and *round*. Old Time Square skirts are usually very large and have sharp corners. Though the sharp corners can be very attractive they are not practical because, with time, they tend to curl. Today's square skirt styles usually have rounded corners and they're not as large as the older skirts. The Old Time Square skirts were sometimes 16 or more inches in size, while today's skirts are usually 12 inches. [this measurement is taken from the top of the skirt, where they are laced together, to the bottom edge]

Round skirts are made in a great variety of shapes and sizes. These can range from a smooth arc, front to back, to the butterfly shape which is larger in the front than the rear and is used commonly on the buckaroo type saddles. The butterfly gives a greater amount of weight distribution in the shoulder area. It is used primarily by ranchers who are roping heavy cattle, which are often larger than their horse. The rounded shape skirts have been the most popular in recent years for most riders and the square shape is appealing for those looking for the nostalgic appearance of the older saddles, particularly those with high cantles.
One of the most important steps in the construction of

POPULAR SKIRT STYLES

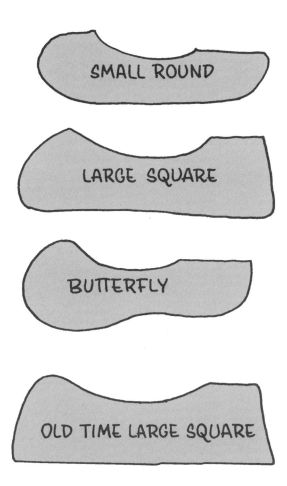

SMALL ROUND

LARGE SQUARE

BUTTERFLY

OLD TIME LARGE SQUARE

SKIRTS

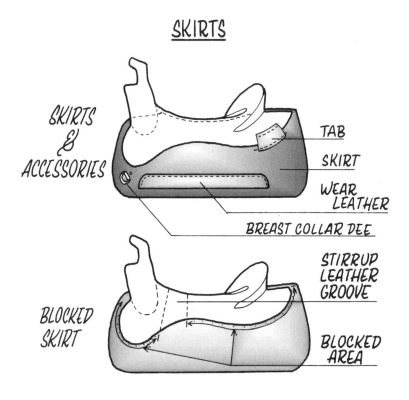

SKIRTS & ACCESSORIES

TAB

SKIRT

WEAR LEATHER

BREAST COLLAR DEE

BLOCKED SKIRT

STIRRUP LEATHER GROOVE

BLOCKED AREA

saddle skirts is the *blocking*. When a saddlemaker "blocks the skirts" the leather is dampened and hand shaped around the entire bar. The blocked skirts are then allowed to dry on the tree. This seats the bars into the skirts and helps the contour of the bars and skirts conform more closely to the shape of the horse's back.

When the blocking is done, and the skirts have dried, they are removed from the tree and leather *plugs* are glued in. [some saddlers call these plugs "Dutchmen"] The purpose of the plug is used to stiffen the skirt leather, which is not under the tree bars, to help distribute some of the rider's weight by creating a larger surface area. The plugs also stiffen the skirts to prevent curling. The blocking is very distinct, even after the plugs are glued in, and can be seen and felt through the sheepskin lining.

Lower quality saddles are usually made without blocking because this takes extra leather, time and effort. Without blocking the tree rides on top of a flat piece of leather. Over a period of use the unblocked skirt leather will try to conform to the shape of the tree, but this is never as satisfactory as a hand blocked skirt. The blocking is very important. Without it the saddle will not sit well and will have a tendency to pitch and roll making it feel like a ship on the ocean. The skirts should always be constructed of good

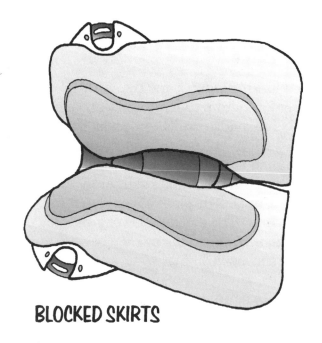

BLOCKED SKIRTS

TREE OUTLINE VISIBLE THROUGH SHEEPSKIN

quality, very thick saddle leather. A top grade saddlemaker chooses skirt leather from the upper back of the hide because of the thickness and uniformity found in that area. The plugs should also be just as thick as the skirts themselves, however, they don't have to be from the same area of the hide. They cannot be porous or "flanky". If low grade leather is used for the plugs the skirts will absorb too much sweat and outside moisture and they will also have a strong tendency to curl.

After the skirts are blocked and plugged the sheepskin lining is applied. The purpose of the sheepskin is to act as a friction surface to help hold the saddle blankets in place. [America seems to be the only country that uses sheepskin. Other areas of the world generally use felt or sueded leather to accomplish the same affect. It is my opinion that sheepskin is used here because, in the early days, it was more readily available in the West than felt material. Our frontiersmen were innovative folks!]

There are two types of sheepskin lining available, *natural* and *synthetic*. Natural sheepskin is *chrome tanned* or *bark tanned*. Chrome tanning should not be used on a horse. It is a process that uses chemicals that might react in a very negative manner when coming in contact with the horse's sweat. The best grade sheepskin is always bark tanned, which is a process using only natural vegetal compounds. It is usually a honey gold color, however, I have seen some chrome tanned sheepskin that was almost white.

The advantage of natural sheepskin is thickness and very good durability (and it feels so good!). It does have some disadvantages. The primary disadvantage is that more than people like it, it also finds favor with insects [such as moths, spiders and crawly things] and four legged things [such as mice, ground squirrels, puppies and kittens]. And these critters can destroy it in a short time. Natural sheepskin must also be installed on each skirt with the grain of the wool going the same direction. When the grain is the wrong direction the saddle blanket will have a tendency to slip out very quickly. If the grain is a different direction on each skirt the blanket will twist under the saddle as you ride.

The advantage of synthetic sheepskin (also called "fake fur") is that it is very inexpensive, has no grain direction and no insects or critters will chew on it. The disadvantage is that it is not very thick and will wear out much faster.

How important is the type and thickness of the sheepskin used? If you have good saddle pads, or blankets, the lining of the skirts is only a minor item. Thick or thin will have no bearing on the rider or the horse. Thick is used because it feels good to the customer and helps sell saddles. I prefer synthetic because it lasts longer and doesn't get "buggy".

While discussing construction of the skirts there is another type that has gained some popularity recently because of the urge to "fit the horse's back". This is a skirt which is lined with a semi-flexible sheet of plastic between the leather and the sheepskin. There is no blocking attempted and even with extended riding no change will occur in the shape around the bars. This type of skirt adjusts it's angles when set on the back of the horse and when you run your hands between the skirt and the horse it feels as though there is a close fit. The problem is, to do this the skirts must be attached to the tree in some fashion that will allow them to pivot. The pressure points, that carry the weight of the saddle and the rider, are these points of pivot attachment. This means that there is less weight distribution and more stress in these areas. The other problem with this "flex" skirt is the positioning on the horse's back. On a broad backed horse most of the weight will be carried on the upper portion of the skirts near the center gullet channel, while on a narrow backed horse these skirts will close in and create an entirely different set of stresses. If the horse is wide near his hips and loin area and narrow at the shoulder this type of skirt will adjust wide in the back and cannot adjust adequately in the front to equalize the pressures created by the pivotal flex. The flexible skirts sound like a good idea, however, they don't work very well in real life except on a very few horses.

One more item that is often found on the skirts is a small dee-ring near the forward edge about one-third of the way up. This is the ring to which the rigging strap of the breast collar is attached. Some saddles have a slot cut through the skirt at this point to be used for the same purpose. I feel that attaching the breast collar to the skirt creates uneven pressures from side to side and that this attachment method often causes wrinkles and distortion in this skirts themselves. This, in turn, will make the saddle set inconsistently and could cause back sores. A better placement for breast collar rings and dee-ring attachment is in the rigging. The flat-plate rigging lends itself to this method very well. With the rigging attached securely to the tree it is unlikely that the pressures applied from the breast collar straps could ever distort them and the pull against the tree would always be equal.

The skirts definitely add weight to the saddle but their function and benefits more than make up for the few additional pounds.

Silver Parade Saddle
(Ted Flowers, circa 1953)
Complete with breast collar, head stall & Garcia Pistol bit
Dusty Johnson Collection

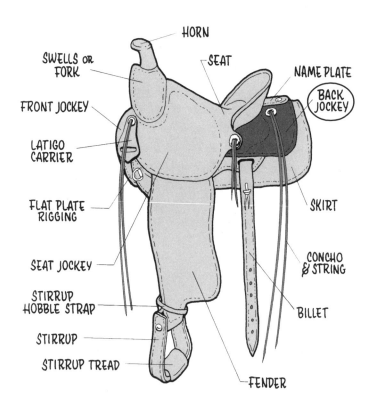

HORN

SWELLS or FORK

SEAT

NAME PLATE

BACK JOCKEY

FRONT JOCKEY

LATIGO CARRIER

FLAT PLATE RIGGING

SKIRT

SEAT JOCKEY

CONCHO & STRING

STIRRUP HOBBLE STRAP

BILLET

STIRRUP

STIRRUP TREAD

FENDER

JOCKEYS

That *jockeys* are the coverings for the exposed parts of the saddle tree bars. They are mostly ornamental but they do offer some protection to the ends of the bars, front and back. Jockeys are also called *housings*.

In the early days saddles had three separate jockeys. This was common on the saddle known as the Texas Trail saddle or the Great Plains saddle from the late 1880's. Over the years the shape of the jockeys changed considerably. The first change was combining the seat and the side jockey into one piece of leather. This left the very front part of the seat [the front jockey] as an individual piece of leather covering the front tips of the bars. Later the side jockey and the front jockey were cut from one piece of leather.

Aside from protecting the bars of the tree the jockey's purpose is to help protect the riders upper legs from the rigging parts and the stirrup straps. The front

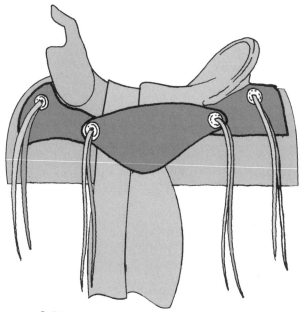

3/4-SEAT SADDLE w/ THREE
SEPARATE JOCKEYS & EIGHT STRINGS

jockeys and the rear jockeys don't interfere with the rider, but they do help to deflect rain and snow and work to prevent foreign materials from getting between the bars and the skirts.

On saddles with in-skirt riggings the rear jockeys are usually built as a part of the skirts. Sometimes these are sewn down solidly and still look like jockeys. In-skirt riggings sometimes have skirts that don't show the back jockeys or the front jockeys. When it appears that the skirts and the jockeys are one piece like this they are known as a Hubbard because they resemble the old Mother Hubbard saddles. The old Mother Hubbard saddles had a single piece of leather covering the seat and the bars and was laced through the center. It appeared as though it was a one piece apron over the entire saddle.

The back jockeys should fit tightly against the rear of the cantle. The back and bottom lines of these housings must also follow the contour of the skirts to give a uniform look. The bottom edge of the rear jockeys should line up with the bottom edge of the front jockey while the back edge of this housing should be pulled down very snugly against the skirts. Sometimes the rear jockeys are connected to (or made a part of) the rear rigging. This looks very strong, but is more for appearance than actual benefit.

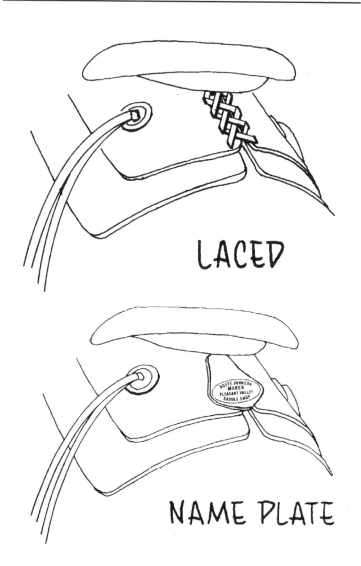

LACED

NAME PLATE

The rear jockeys are usually fastened together in the center with *lacing* or sewn in place with a piece of leather called a plate, or *nameplate*. This usually carries the name of the maker, however, it sometimes has the name or brand of the saddle owner.

These jockeys are held in place with the *saddle strings*. These leather strips are normally 3/8" to 1/2" wide. These "strings" pass through the jockeys, the trees and the skirts. They anchor all of the saddle parts together.

Saddles that have a separate front jockey are called an *eight-string saddle* because there are four individual strings on each side. A *six-string saddle* [the most common today] does not have the concho and string at the base of the fork. That concho and string have been replaced by a small screw because the front jockey is now a part of the seat.

Today many saddles have no strings at all. They have been replaced by conchos with a screw back or a decorative screw which secures a small D ring. The saddle string and concho method of construction is definitely more secure.

The jockeys add nothing to the security and safety of the saddle but they are very visible and should be made from very nice leather, decorated attractively and fit well.

Rear jockeys have been known to be the home of all
sorts of strange pockets. Some of the early saddles
had saddlebags fastened permanently to the jockeys.
On rare occassion these saddle pockets were even
covered with fur (angora goat or bear were most
popular). Later it was popular to have a hoofpick
pocket sewn on the left rear jockey. I have even seen
pistol holsters and knife sheaths afixed here. I believe
that anything fastened to the jockeys in a permanent
fashion will soon become a permanent annoyance! It
is bound to get in the way and become just another
gimmick that will get snagged and torn. Do yourself a
favor and keep the rear jockeys smooth and attractive.
You'll be glad you did!

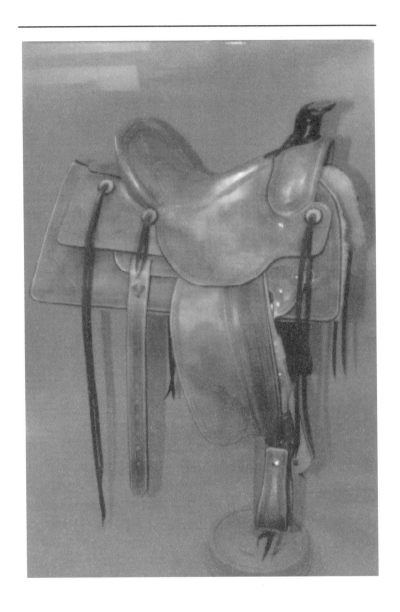

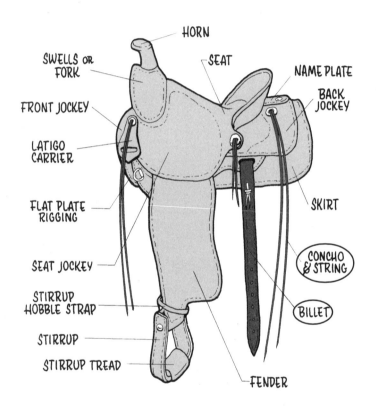

HORN

SWELLS or FORK

SEAT

NAME PLATE

BACK JOCKEY

FRONT JOCKEY

LATIGO CARRIER

FLAT PLATE RIGGING

SKIRT

SEAT JOCKEY

CONCHO & STRING

STIRRUP HOBBLE STRAP

BILLET

STIRRUP

STIRRUP TREAD

FENDER

CINCHAS, LATIGOS, CONCHOS & STRINGS

Cincha, meaning "girth," is the Spanish word for *cinch*. A cinch is the wide band that goes under the horse's belly to hold the saddle in position. The purpose of the cinch is to anchor the saddle to the horse as comfortably as possible. The cinch should not interfere with the horse's action. Cinches are made of webbing, cords, canvas, leather, and nylon.

The cinch is one of the most "taken for granted" items of the saddle. The important elements of the cinch are: the <u>size</u>, the <u>rings</u> and the <u>materials</u>.

The *size* refers to both length and width. The general rule for length is that the rings should be approximately 12" below the rigging plates. Cinches can be ordered any length, with the common sizes being 30", 32" and 34". They are measured from the outside of the ring on one end to the outside of the ring on the other end.

The other measurement of size is the *width* of the
cinch. The width should vary according to the
position of the rigging plates as follows;
>full position — 17 strand cinch
>7/8 position — 19 strand cinch
>3/4 position — 21 strand cinch

Using a cinch that is wider than necessary in any
position would extend too far forward and the foreleg
of the horse would be constantly rubbing on it, which
would result in chafing and sores in that area.

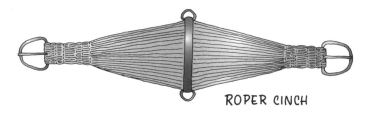

ROPER CINCH

Super-wide roping cinches have become popular in
recent years. Wide cinches have their place when
roping heavy cattle and should not be pulled very tight
except while roping. They have no place on the
pleasure or trail horse. Most riders think that this wide

cinch is more humane and doesn't cut into "Old Dobbin", but the truth is that the wider cinch must be pulled tighter to hold the saddle as well and this tightness creates a corset effect across the horse's chest. Restricted breathing is not a desireable trait! It is much better to have the right size cinch and not have to tighten it so much!

At each end of the cinch is the *ring*. This is used to run the latigos through when tying to the saddle. There are three styles of rings: round ring, ring with-buckle-tongue, and ring with-crossbar. The round ring is found on the cheapest of cinches and can only be used by tying the latigo. The round ring with-buckle-tongue is an improvement because it eliminates the bulk of a cinch knot, however, when the tongue is attached at the bottom of the ring it is also considered cheap. This arrangement can become ineffective if the pressures on the ring should make it oval. When the ring becomes oval the tongue goes through the ring and doesn't work to lock the latigo in place. I see many riders using this type of ring with a knot and allowing the tongue to hang loose. This is a potential hazard to man and horse!

The best cinch ring is the ring with-crossbar. The crossbar prevents the ring from being pulled into an oval and the tongue is much shorter and less hazardous. The ideal ring with-crossbar is made with a flat profile (more surface area distributes pressure wider), a flat

---

top surface (prevents unnecessary distortion of the latigo) and a small tab on the inside bottom prevents the cords from bunching to either side of the ring. This ideal ring is made of stainless steel. Another very acceptable material is bronze. Any cinch ring constructed of plain iron or iron with nickle or chrome plating should be avoided because of rust problems.

BUCKLES

(avoid this style)   **(Best overall design)**

The *materials* in a cinch are very important. In bygone days the cinches were made of horsehair. The best were from mane hair and the poor grades were from tail hair. These were very durable and seemed to work quite well, but didn't do much to absorb moisture. Other old time cinches were made of canvas or burlap.

Horses get sores because of heat and moisture! The ideal cinch promotes transference of sweat away from the body and allows evaporation to cool and dry the heated area.

The best material to transfer water is cotton, but cotton looses much of its strength when wet. The next best is *mohair*. Mohair is a blend of Angora Goat hair and Wool. It transfers water (sweat) rapidly AND becomes stronger with the addition of moisture. Mohair is also the best cinch material because it cleans easily and is best washed with mild soap (Ivory, dish soap, etc.) and water. [Be sure to rinse out all soap before putting back on the horse] Mohair cinches are expensive, but not excessively so and will last a very long time. Some are created with 20% nylon added to reduce the price. These are also very good, but do not equal the pure mohair cinch.

Many cinches are made of 100% nylon, or other synthetic, cord. While these are strong they will not absorb or transfer moisture and will create a certain amount of heat.

Another popular style is the *nylon strap cinch with fleece covering*.

FLEECE LINED CINCH

These are widely seen in arena situations (ie. rodeos, horseshow, cutting contests) but are not practical for general riding due to their tendency to collect burrs, stickers and other foreign matter. Also, the fleece makes for a lot of heat and moisture.

In my opinion, the worst possible cinch is the neoprene rubber cinch. This type is usually made of nylon and is either covered with a rubber sleeve or has the neoprene rubber stitched to the horse side. They cannot breathe, create great heat and moisture and cause chafing very quickly. I believe they have become popular because they are easy to clean, look "hi-tech" and feel soft to the <u>rider's</u> hands. Softness is not the quest. The horse needs ventilation!

A good cinch should have a cross-bar (usually nylon) stitched in the enter with D rings on each side. These are to use with tie-downs, breast collars and connecting straps. These D's should also be made of stainless steel or bronze to avoid rust and corrosion.

It is common for the center of the cord cinch to have a diamond pattern woven in the center and a triangle at each ring. I also like a narrow bar across the section between the diamond and the triangle to prevent the cords from becoming tangled. This cross-bar should always be centered under the horse's belly.

Latigos and Billets

Latigo is the name of a specific type of oil-tanned leather (usually, but not always, burgundy color). In the case of a saddle the word Latigo refers to the tie straps that connect the saddle and the cinch. It is cut from top grade latigo leather and should be 1 1/2" to 2" wide and about 6' long. It is then laced to the near (left) side rigging ring and laced through the cinch ring to be tied or buckled. The excess length is then hung in the *latigo keeper*, which is a tab of leather with a slot that is fastened near the front jockey. Sometimes this "latigo" is made of nylon or other synthetic

BILLETS   materials.

On the off (right) side of the saddle another latigo may be used, however, it is more common to see a *doubled billet*. It will be the same width and about 5' long with holes for buckling the cinch tongue. Sometimes these tie straps are made of nylon which causes some heat and slips quite a bit. The advantage to nylon is strength and ease of maintainence. They are still referred to as Latigos.

BACK
BILLET

From the back of the rigging hang the *back* or *rear billets*. These are 1 1/2" to 2" wide and about 3' long with holes for buckling to the rear cinch. They are laced in place through slots or metal D's. They are made of a single layer of leather or doubled (lined) with a second piece. The doubling is only for show.

Additional strength is not required here.

The *rear cinch*, or *flank cinch*, is seen on most western saddles and is useless in most cases! It has nothing to do with how well a saddle stays in place for most riding situations. Its purpose is to prevent the back of the saddle from tilting upward when roping. Because they

FLANK CINCH

come with most saddles riders feel they must use them.

Consider ... most riders leave the flank cinch hang down about 3". In the position where they will contact the horse the belly is soft and will compress about 6" when pushed upward. Added together this means that the saddle will tilt up 9 to 10" before stopping. Will that really help a rider maintain his seat?? The other problem with rear cinches is many people allow them to hang even lower where a horse can catch a hoof in it or a big weed can become lodged between it and the soft belly. Either event will make things get a little more "western" than most riders desire. If the cinch is pulled up as tight as should be it, effectively, makes the saddle become a <u>brace</u> across the horse's back and stops much of the flexability that is needed for smooth action.

I have heard riders proclaim that the flank cinch is used to keep the saddle in place when riding downhill. If the angle of the cinch is proper there is no way that it can contribute to holding back the forward slide. The only proper attachment for this purpose is a *crupper*. A crupper goes around the base of the tail and is buckled to the back of the saddle.

Saddle Strings and Conchos

SADDLE-STRING ASSEMBLY

Saddle strings hold together the pieces of the saddle covering. The complete assembly consist of the saddle string (usually 3/8" latigo straps) and two conchos. The top concho may be of either leather or metal. The both ends of the string begin between the sheepskin and the skirt leather, continues through two holes in the tree and exits up through the jockey. The conchos are then slipped on to act as a washer and the string is tied by the slit-braid tie method which makes for a very solid and attractive assembly.

The strings should be long (26" to 36") and strong

CROSS SECTION OF A SADDLE-STRING ASSEMBLY THROUGH THE TREE

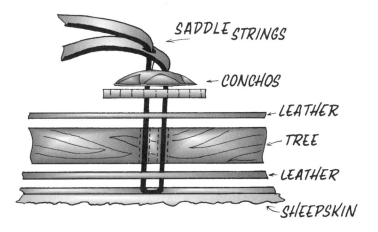

SADDLE STRINGS
← CONCHOS
← LEATHER
← TREE
← LEATHER
← SHEEPSKIN

enough to tie on slickers, medicine bags, canteens, etc. Old time saddles always had long strings, however, ropers are in the habit of tying them up short to keep them from interferring with their swing.

As the need for strings diminished (and construction costs were cut) strings disappeared from many rigs. They are replaced with a screw-and-washer which goes through the concho. Because riders still occassionally need to tie things on, sometimes, a dee-ring is afixed under the screw. A more decorative way to do this and eliminate the string is to use a screw with an engraved silver concho over the leather concho. This is not as strong a method of assembly but is acceptable for pleasure saddles.

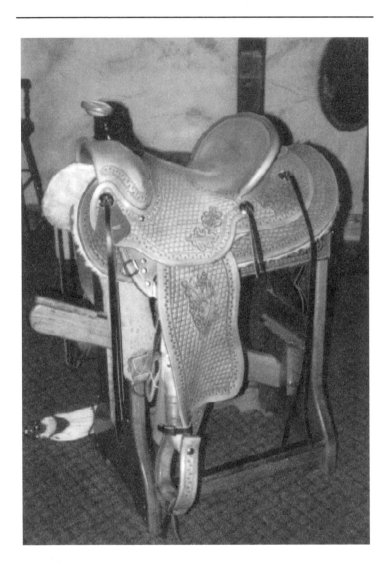

SADDLE BLANKETS
&
PADS

A good saddle blanket or pad is absolutely essential to protect the horse's back. It is placed on the horse's back under the saddle. Its primary purpose is to protect the back from sharp digs and gouges created by uneven weight distribution on the saddle. It must also help remove water and cool the back. All of this is a lot to expect from a small piece of material, so it is imperative that the pad be chosen carefully.

There is no saddle, no matter how well made, that can fit properly for the entire life of the horse! Physical changes occur in all living things as time progresses. The horse's basic conformation remains the same but his body will make many changes throughout his life. All horses have one side less well developed than the other. When the rider is mounted the saddle will tend to roll to the less-developed side. This puts constant pressure and stress on the weakest area and interferes with proper blood flow and certain reflex centers. This discomfort will cause him to pull away from the pressured area and not perform up to his full potential. Obviously, it is imperative to deflect the impact on a horse's muscles and reflex centers. A good pad should never allow the bars, which are carrying the rider's weight, to exert constant pressure against the muscles. The pad should be resilient and should reconform as the animal moves.

The elements to look for in a good pad are: *comfort*, *durability* and adequate *protection* for the horse's back. To determine what pad properly meets these criteria first consider the type of riding that it will be used for. How many hours a day will it be used? Are there any special demands in the activities you ride in?

Which blanket?

A cutting horse requires a thin, natural fiber pad that provides enough cushion to keep the horse comfortable without hindering his performance. He is usually only ridden for short periods of time and allowed to cool between usages.

A roper will want maximum shock absorption. Extra bulk may be acceptable to protect a horse's back when the steer hits the end of the rope, jarring the saddle bars into his back.

An endurance rider requires a pad that is light, will cover the minimum surface area below the skirts and has a highly breathable surface in order to not trap heat and moisture.

The pleasure rider needs a light pad that will do a superior job of distributing rider and saddle weight evenly across a horse's back while riding in a wide variety of conditions.

The priority is to keep the animal comfortable and sound throughout many demanding conditions. The key elements in all of the above uses are <u>shock absorption and minimizing heat and moisture buildup.</u>

Saddle Pad

Materials

Next, consider the materials. The materials in a pad greatly influence its performance characteristics. They are classified in two categories: natural fibers and synthetics. Natural fibers are cotton, wool, and mohair.

The synthetics include nylon, rayons, rubber and plastics.

Wool and wool/mohair blends are the prime choice in natural pads and blankets for several reasons. It is cool, it breaths and readily conforms to the back without compressing too much. The natural crimp of the individual strands of fleece and mohair give it a functional springiness. The wool fibers allow air to pass which helps cool the animal's back. Additionally, they wick water away quickly and adhere well to horsehair, which helps reduce slippage. The cushioning effect of the wool will help compensate for minor fitting problems by conforming to the horse's back and improving weight distribution.

1" Felt Pad

I prefer a 1" grey felt pad, however, 3/4" can also be very effective, particularly when used with a light woolen saddle blankct on top. Care must be taken to not let the padding become too thick as this would make the saddle rock back and forth like a ship on the ocean. Care must also be exercise to insure that the pads and blankets do not bunch up under the bars. Bunching and wrinkling would be the same as a small stick or pebble in your shoe. It can only get worse as time goes on! Wool and mohair blankets must be washed periodically to maintain their softness and breathability. They must also be regularly inspected due to their tendency to snag burrs and weeds in their fibers.

While natural pads are always good, there are also some excellent synthetic pads. Recent developments have produced some synthetic materials with improved wicking ability, better heat dissipaton, and better cushioning properties than have ever been available in the past. A good example of this is the high quality synthetic orthopedic felt used in hospitals for burn and bedridden patients. This same material is being used in many saddle pads.

Synthetic is not always good, though. The synthetic fleece pads compact too much, create heat, do not breathe and slip excessively. The rubberized pads do not slip, but they also do not wick moisture, create great heat and compress more than necessary. Their only advantage seems to be that they clean easily.

There are also pads being manufactured that are said to be "self conforming" due to various fluids and gels inserted into the pads. These would definitely absorb shock from the saddle and rider, but they retain heat. Heat causes moisture, and rubbing against moist hair and flesh causes sores.

The best synthetic pad I have been exposed to has an open mesh top and an insert of closed-cell foam shaped to fit only under the bars. The closed-cell foam doesn't collapse like the spongy open cell foams. This shaped foam has a great number of small holes which allow the heat and moisture to escape while it is conforming to the shape of the animal's back. Between this foam and the horse's back is a 1/4" layer of open-cell foam and beneath it is a very light layer of brushed nylon. This combination gives excellent breathability and cushioning. It is, however, unusual looking and not readily accepted by Western riders who insist upon remaining with traditional saddle blankets.

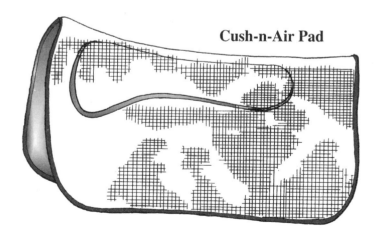

Cush-n-Air Pad

The manufacturers have offered this pad with a wool top just for these "traditional" people, but the extra layer defeats much of the beneficial effect of this design.

Avoid pads that have waves in the material and avoid those that have small knots or lumps in the fabric. These can cause pressure points that will lead to trouble.

Too lumpy

Wear leathers have been used for many years. These are small strips of thin leather sewn onto the edges of the pad to help prevent excessive wear under the constant swing of the stirrup leathers. This is a very

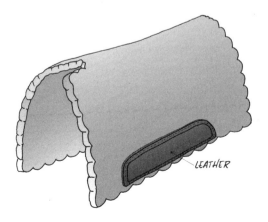

LEATHER

good idea, but like many good ideas it has been taken too far. Many companies are making wear leathers thicker and thicker to enable them to do ornate carving and set silver conchos. These are certainly attractive and look great on a saddle stand, but they also widen the ride. Up to this point we have been trying to "get closer to the horse". The heavy wear leathers defeat this for the sake of appearance!

A top grade pad should also be made to fit the contour of the back. The pad should have extra material over the withers and across the back edge. This will cause a folded pad to have a definite upward arch along the fold. This will lessen the pressure caused when the saddle is cinched down.

Pad problems

The most common padding problem is simply overpadding! Too much bulk is worse than not enough as it completely changes the fit of the saddle. By perching the saddle way up above the withers the saddle becomes unstable. The creates continuous weight distribution and pressure changes (remember the "little girl in the backpack?") Also this causes a need to overtighten the cinch to compensate.

Too much padding causes more of that dreaded heat, inteferes with evaporation and keeps the skin from breathing naturally. If you need more than two layers of pad and blanket you should rethink your method of padding and the reasons for what you are doing.

It is not possible to make a poor saddle fit better by adding more pads. If the saddle is too tight for your horse no amount of padding will correct it. If the problem is the gullet being too close (touching?) the withers consider using a bottom pad with the wither area removed from the pad.

Cleanliness is another common problem. Felt and wool pads tend to hold horsehair, along with burrs and twigs, and a buildup of these foreign materials will affect fit. If the blankets and pads are clean they will also have much more cushion and can do their job. Dirt clods, no matter how small, will dig into the horse. Pads that have been very wet and dry under the saddle will have compressed areas that have lost their spring. Riding with a dirty blanket is no better than wearing Italian shoes with dirty socks!

The size of the blanket is another potential problem. It should show at least 1" all around the skirts. This means tht the blanket or pad should be at least two inches longer than the length of the skirt and two inches wider than the underside width of the skirts. Some companies today are offerring pads and blankets that are so large that they extend 4" to 6" beyond the saddle leather. This is also bad because it causes heat, prevents the saddle from sitting in place properly and keeps the rider's legs out and away from the horse.

You can see that the pad is just as important as the saddle in order to get optimum performance from your horse. Choose your saddle pads and blankets carefully, use them properly and keep them clean.

Miniature Saddle -approx 20" tall
(Jack Thomas - circa 1975)
Complete with headstall, lariat, silver bit & silver conchos
John Bianchi Collection

BUYING
A
SADDLE

When deciding to purchase a saddle many options are available. While price and decoration are important factors they must not be the primary reasons for choice. I believe that appropriateness for intended use, comfort for horse and rider, quality of materials and durability of construction should come first. These factors apply to *custom* saddles, *manufactured* saddles and *used* saddles. Though there are large differences in these three catagories they must all adhere to the same principles. However, different expectations also apply.

CUSTOM SADDLES

The first consideration in choosing a custom saddle is finding a skilled saddlemaker who you have confidence in. Reputation is the first indication to seek. When a maker developes a good reputation it is not by accident. It means he (or she) has worked hard to produce the very best product with excellent materials and that product has withstood the test of a variety of horsemen and skill levels. This is not to say that a newcomer to the saddlemaking trade cannot make an excellent rig, but that newcomer's workmanship must be evaluated with more care.

If possible try to visit the custom saddle shops in your area to personally evaluate their workmanship and styles. Obtain as many custom catalogs as possible. Always compare construction and workmanship. Keep in mind that a "name" isn't always the same person who built the saddle. Many times a big "name" has been licensed to the manufacturer and today's products may not be as good as the original.

When you order a custom saddle you will be asked to specify many dimensions, i.e.: seat size, cantle height, fork style and width, type of bars, horn style and size, etc., etc.. Any good custom maker will be glad to help you decide what will work best for you.

Always ask about the type of leather that will be used. At the time of this writing the finest saddle leathers come from U.S. tanneries. Imported leather, particularly that from Mexico and South America, is generally undesireable and shows that corners are being cut for the sake of price. This can only lead to questioning what other corners may be cut at the sacrifice of quality and durability.

Expect to place a non-refundable deposit. The maker must order a tree (which can take up to 3 months for delivery) and pay for it in advance. He must also order hardware and leather for your job. Once the leather is cut it is difficult to use it on another saddle.

A typical custom saddle requires approximately 35 to 50 hours to construct, longer if heavily decorated. Layers of damp leather are used and drying times must be factored into the construction time. A top-grade saddle maker can usually deliver your custom rig in 3 to 8 months, depending on his work load. If the wait is much longer either you are dealing with a maker in the top 5% of the trade or he is devoting time to other projects and not entirely concentrating on making new custom saddles.

The cost of a custom saddle will be fairly close from shop to shop. The best materials cost each shop the same and a good craftsman must expect fair payment for his experience, skill and overhead. Large deviations in price should be carefully examined. In other words, don't expect to find any "bargains" in a good custom saddle. I have never been able to understand why any horseman will pay $25,000 for a pickup that will depreciate and wear out in 8 years and, at the same time, balk at $2,500 for a custom saddle that will probably last for a couple of generations!

MANUFACTURED SADDLES

Factory produced saddles are basically machine made
in a mass-production environment. The parts are
machine cut with steel dies and designs are embossed
with huge hydraulic presses. One or two workers do
each type of operation, in assembly line style, before
the saddle is passed over to the next team. No one
individual builds the entire saddle and it is unlikely
that the same quality standards apply to each part.

Construction is sometimes very good and many of
these saddles are just as strong as most custom outfits,
however, many factory-made saddles have surprisingly
poor construction. These will be evident by the use of
low-grade leather, cheap buckles and rigging plates,
plastic stirrups and the use of staples in place of nails
and screws.

Many of these manufactured rigs are dressed up with
"silver" corners, trim and conchos and have beautiful
carving. This carving is not accomplished by hand,
but is first embossed hydraulically and then some of
the edges are dressed-up by hand. This gives additional
depth and makes it appear as though all the work was
done by a skilled leathercarver.

Even though most manufacturers offer a variety of sizes
and styles the purchaser has very few options due to

the limited variations in molded (synthetic) trees and die-cut leather (or synthetic) parts. Careful observation will reveal that the wide variety offered is mostly cosmetic. Some catalogs offer a wider variety of "options" on their more expensive models, but these are not custom built saddles.

Manufacturers often employ professional ropers, barrel racers, rodeo stars, etc. to endorse their saddles. These "Pros" usually offer some assistance with design of a particular saddle, or line of saddles, but they have nothing to do with production or quality control.

Some manufactured saddles are excellent but more fall off the other end of the scale. The best advice, if you intend to purchase a factory made saddle, is to evaluate it carefully, have it examined by an expert and don't expect to get more than you paid for.

USED SADDLES

Buying a new saddle can be a really enjoyable experience, however it can also sometimes be more than the budget will allow at the time. Purchasing a used saddle is usually the only answer to saving money on tack and it can save hundreds of dollars. Be careful! Sometimes that "bargain" can end up costing lots of repair dollars and veterinarian fees.

Let's look at some basic guidelines for evaluating a used rig before purchase.

First, of course, is evaluation of the tree. Is it's width right for your horse? Is it solid? A broken tree cannot be made whole again, even if it is repaired. No matter how nice the rest of the saddle is if the tree is broken you should walk away. How do you check for this? Put the saddle down on its horn and press downward on the cantle ... hard! If it is broken you will feel the flex and you might even hear popping sounds. Pass that test? Now lay it on its side and press against the bars. Same thing, if it flexes walk away!

Look under the jockeys at the ends. Is the rawhide firm and tight or is it cracked, peeling and has the lacing going bad? (expensive to repair) How about the leather throughout? Is it dry or is it deeply cracked? If it is dry you can oil it, but if it is cracked it is not going to heal. If it feels too oily and is very dark maybe the seller is trying to cover up the fact that it has been abused in the past.

Is the leather worn out in any special places? Heavy abrasion on the horn and fork indicates hard roping. Thin seat jockeys indicate lots of riding. A loose and wiggly Cheyenne-roll indicates poor construction and being carried and lifted too many times by the cantle. This cannot be firmed up again without a major expense. Also be sure to check that the stitching on the cantle binding isn't loose or worn.

Badly curled skirts indicate lack of care and, probably, improper storing. They will need to be flattened as much as possible to eliminate lumps that could cause back sores. Check the sheepskin lining. Does it need replacing? Worn sheepskin shows that the saddle was well used. Sheepskin with holes indicates bugs and/or mice have been working on it. Perhaps they have also worked on other important areas?

Are the saddle strings in good shape, broken, hard or missing altogether? They must be replaced for convenience and security of saddle construction.

The rigging is extremely important. Is is secure? Look for cracks, tears and heavy wear. Are the rivets and nails firmly intact? How about the screws fastening it to the tree? Pay close attention here as this is a safety item!

Look over the entire length of the stirrup leathers. Are they firm, flexible and supple? Again, a safety item. They can be replaced without too much expense, but always check them. At the same time, check the other straps. The flank cinch, billets, latigos, off billets and cinch. Worn or bent buckles must be replaced.

Finally, check the stirrups. Are the covers still intact? Be sure the stirrups are not broken or twisted. They can be replaced, but this is another expense on that "bargain" saddle. Be sure there is a stirrup hobble included. Remember, this is another safety item.

Carefully review the chapter about seats. Does it have enough room and do you feel good sitting in it?

Finally, if you are not sure of your own judgement and experience take the saddle to a professional and get his opinion. Please remember that most trainers are pretty good at evaluating the fit of a saddle, but they are not saddlemakers and usually cannot truly evaluate construction and material quality in saddles. Go to a saddlemaker for his opinion and pay him a fair fee to examine the saddle. It is worth a few dollars to get an expert opinion before you spend a lot of dollars on a saddle that will not give you the service you expect.

If you still have questions ask permission to try it on your horse. This is one advantage when buying a used saddle. Rarely will a custom saddle shop or a tack store allow you to ride a brand new saddle because once it is scratched from normal riding it can never be sold as new to another customer.

The used saddle, however, can usually be "tried out". Most reasonable folks will allow you to try it out on your own horse. This does not mean riding it for a week and bringing it back dirty and scratched. It means checking it for fit and comfort, period!!

Bargains are worth looking for, but always be cautious.

SADDLE CARE

With proper care, leather is extremely durable. As leather prices continue to rise, so does the resale value of leather items. A used, 20 year old saddle can often be sold for its original price or more if it is in good condition.

Cleaning and conditioning will not help much if the saddle is mistreated on a regular basis. It should be protected from excessive or prolonged wetting. This could soften the rawhide on the tree or cause the surface leather to stretch. When it dries it is liable to crack and the evaporation of water takes the oils with it.

Avoid extreme heat, such as the trunk of your car or in a window exposed to sunlight for long periods. Store the saddle in a dry place on a saddle stand. Saddles are intended to fit horses and tend to curl up when put on something much narrower like a fence rail or sawhorse. Leather has a "memory" and tends to curl up and stay that way. Once it is badly curled there is not much that can be done about it.

Do not allow the stirrups to touch the floor as the fenders may be bent out of shape. When stored the stirrups should be twisted into a riding position and held that way with a stick through them both (a broomstick works fine). Never allow any leather to touch the floor during storage because it allows small "critters" to crawl up the saddle and do damage to the leather and sheepskin. When the saddle is in storage always cover it to keep off the dust. Dust can settle into the pores and damage leather over a period of time.

Never lay the saddle on the ground. If it must lay on the ground for a short time it should be laid on its side with the fenders and stirrup leathers laying smoothly in a natural position. If the sheepskin is allowed to touch ground it can pick up sticks, dirt and debris, all of which are hard to clean off and can be even harder on a horse's back.

Tanned leather won't last long without regular cleaning, conditioning and protection from the elements. The most important cleaning tools are time and elbow-grease. Regular care makes cleaning and conditioning a short job, but let it go and it will be a half-day chore!

Saddle Stands

Front View   Back View

Well designed stand giving maximum support to skirts

(Photos courtesy Wooden Horse Wood Products, Pulaski, PA.)

Folding Stand

Folding stands are usually made of 1" tube. Give
adequate support but may allow stirrups to rest
on floor.

A number of good products are available today, but beware of anything that claims to "clean, condition and protect" in one operation. Logic will tell you that this cannot truly be so. The best products are individually formulated to work together to meet all three of these basic requirements ... without causing damage to the leather.

CLEANING

Cleaning removes dirt, sweat and other damaging substances from the surface of the leather. The oil in the leather naturally attracts dirt! A good cleaning agent  breaks down the oil to remove the dirt. Most soaps are alkaline and may damage leather if left on for any length of time. Most soaps intended for leather contain glycerine to begin conditioning while removing oils.

I cannot recommend saddle soaps because they contain too many fats which are liable to plug up the pores of the leather and not allow the dirt to be washed out while cleaning. I make a lather from a bar of Ivory soap and scrub my saddle with it. First, wipe the saddle with a wet cloth, then work in the Ivory lather and flush with a very wet cloth. Liberal water is needed to flush away the dirt. It makes no sense to just move the dirt from place to place.

Use a well rung-out sponge or rag so that the excess water doesn't carry the alkaline soap deeply into the fibers. Rinse the sponge frequently and use clear water to wipe away excess soap lather.

Give an extra washing to the areas that have come in contact with sweat, such as the underside of the cinch strap, the back side of the fenders and stirrup leathers, the flank cinch and the billets. Allow the saddle to dry at room temperature. Never allow it to dry in direct sun or too close to a heater as this will cause the leather surface to shrink and make it crack. Once it cracks it cannot be repaired.

Once leather fibers have become brittle and dry, all the oiling and conditioning in the world will not make it stong again. If the leather has a deep cracks or is powdery, it is gone. You may be able to make it look better, but it will never be whole again. One way to judge the leather's strength is to twist it severely back and forth. Pull at the stitches and try to tear them . If they tear apart they are rotted beyond repair. Further, if you can damage the leather in any way with your bare hands you don't want to trust it and must consider it unsafe to use.

Mildew is one of those good news, bad news affairs. On one hand, mildew's presence means there are still oils in your leather. You never find mildew on leather that has been completely dried out. On the other hand, it is a sign that destructive molds are at work. It's presence is made known by either a white powder or a blue-green "sticky" surface, particularly around brass fittings and rivets. An excellent way to get rid of it is to use *white vinegar* straight from the bottle. Sponge the entire surface of the leather, applying heavier over the offending areas. Repeat until the mildew is gone. Rinse out with clear water and thoroughly wash the leather with Ivory soap to minimize any damage the vinegar may have done. Set aside to thoroughly dry before applying conditioner. Be sure to keep this saddle in a very dry area to prevent this from happening again.

CONDITIONING

Since cleaning removes most oil, the next step is to replace the saddle's oil and rejuvenate the leather. Leather conditioners restore softness, flexibility and strength. You can test a conditoner by applying a small amount to the back of your hand. If it feels sticky or greasy, it will attract dirt and probably won't be absorbed into the leather. If it burns your hand, it will burn the leather, too.

Unlike cleaning, leather conditioning should only be done periodically depending on the amount of use and climate that the saddle is exposed to. Over-conditioning will not make it stronger or better. There is only so much oil that a piece of leather can absorb. Too much oil can cause the leather to become mushy and allow the fibers to detach from each other. This makes the leather weak and unsafe.

Before I talk about what conditioners to use, let me tell you what NOT to use. Please never, never, never use bacon grease, motor oil, lard, unsalted butter, olive oil or any type of food product. Food products (olive oil, lard, etc.) will live in the fibers of the leather and will begin to decompose (turn rancid) in warm weather. This rancid action will rot the leather, too. Remember, leather is *skin* — dried meat — and anything that is in contact with it will transfer its rotting bacteria easily to the internal fibers. Never try to condition with anything that is based on a food product!

My longtime favorite leather dressing is 100% pure neatsfoot oil. This old standby for leather conditioning was produced by boiling cattle hooves and skimming off the oil. True neatsfoot oil is no longer available. Every can that has "neatsfoot" on its label does not contain the same product. Products with this name now on the market are actually blends of various fats and oils such as lard oil and petroleum based oils.

Manufacturers are reluctant to reveal their formulas, however, some contain animal-based oils such as mink oil, lanolin and fish oils. Others contain plant-derived oils, primarily vegetable oils, while still others are based on beeswax. They have a variety of consistencies and spreading rates.

Always use *"pure"* neatsfoot oil. Neatsfoot labeled *"compound"* contains a mixture of animal fat with petroleum-based mineral oils. Petroleum oils are not the bogeymen many people have made them out to be. They do not rot stitching any more than other leather care products do. However, they do tend to darken the leather very much! They also tend to "spread" indefinitely. While vegetable oils bond with leather and stay put, mineral oils do not. The excess oil will end up on your hands, clothing and other places you probably don't want it.

Avoid the compound and always stay with "pure" neatsfoot oils. Each saddlemaker and tanner usually has a favorite conditioner, however, they all agree that they should be made of animal - not vegetable - fat since they most closely resemble the natural moisturizers that the cow originally produced for himself.

Soaking in and "spreadability" are the important factors in any conditioner. A simple way to test an oil is to rub a little into a piece of dry leather and see if it disappears from the surface. If it does, it has been absorbed into the leather and will spread throughout, if not, it will only provide a superficial protection that will not last long and may clog the pores of the leather.

The most efficient way to apply an oil product is to pour it into a small bowl and then paint it on with a small brush. Another applicator that works well is a sheepskin swab with fairly short nap. The oil should be warm when applied. I put my neatsfoot in a plastic cola bottle and heat that in a waterfilled crockpot. This makes the oil thin so that it soaks in immediately. Be very careful if you heat on a stove or hot plate. Most oils will begin to smoke and burst into flame at about 140 degrees. This is very hazardous and dangerous to be around and oil this hot will actually damage the leather. The mild heating in a crockpot is quite safe and leaves the thin oil still easily worked with bare hands.

Apply the oil in thin coats. Let it soak into the leather for a while and then go back over it again. Two or three light coats will spread nicely and penetrate much better than fully soaking the leather. After the last coat, go back over the entire saddle with a dry cloth to wipe off any excess.

(A short side note: ... Be sure to pull the stirrup leathers
part way out and oil where they bend around the bars.
Most folks forget to do this and this is an area that
takes a lot of stress. DON'T pull the leathers out all
the way as it is very difficult to get them back in place!)

PROTECTION

After the conditioner has had time to spread evenly
(usually overnight) some form of surface protection
must be applied. This is a step that is frequently
overlooked. If some sort of sealer is not applied the
oils will dry out fairly quickly and dust and dirt will
work into the fibers of the leather.

Avoid any kind of finish that is sticky as this will attract
dirt and will soil your clothing each time you ride.
Examples of the finishes NOT to use are: mink oil/
wax products, snow seal, waterproof waxes, etc.

Most natural waxes such as beeswax can be used if
applied very sparingly. Never allow them to cake up
in carved or stamped leather. This not only looks
bad, but it chokes off any air or oil that could be
beneficial to the leather. Acrylic and resin finishes
can be used, if they can be removed by washing with
mild soaps.

The worst thing you can do to leather is apply a lacquer

finish of some type. First, lacquer seals the grain surface and the leather cannot breathe. Second, the lacquer will have to be stripped before any leather conditioner can be applied again, and this requires the use of acetone or some type of lacquer thinner. These harsh substances will permanently damage the surface of the leather. The commercial names of products of this type give themselves away. A simple rule in my saddle shop is "If it ends in -lac, put it back".

I prefer simple, flexible wax finishes. Some companies make these in liquid form and others offer them in spray containers. New products are being introduced almost weekly. Before using them always try a sample on a small piece of leather and test for ease of removal and affect it will have on leather color.

A very beautiful and mellow finish can be had by simply using a bar of pure glycerine. (Yes, the same glycerine bar you used to clean the saddle) By polishing with glycerine on a slightly damp cloth, you will put on a very mellow shine and provide an oil free surface that doesn't attract dust and dirt. Be very careful to have your cloth "dry" when polishing over the carving and stamping or you'll defeat your previous cleaning work by clogging all of the deep areas with the glycerine residue.

Don't neglect the tie-straps, latigos and saddle strings

while doing this cleaning and conditioning. These items are more exposed to sweat and salt than the rest of the saddle and need excellent care to extend their useful life.

How frequently should all of this be done?? If you ride daily, in addition to wiping off the saddle daily with a damp cloth, it should be thoroughly cleaned every 6 to 8 weeks if your area is average in humidity. More frequently if it is very dry. If your saddle becomes extremely wet (downpour, fording a stream, leak in the roof of the barn) the cleaning and oiling procedure should begin immediately. A thin coat of leather dressing will slow down the drying procedure and will help prevent curling. When it has gotten back to dry condition proceed as you would after a normal cleaning.

If you only ride occassionally, the leather treatments need only be done twice a year. If your saddle sits on a rack in your home as only a display an annual treatment should be adequate.

A well built saddle that is cared for consistently should outlast many horses. It may even outlast the owner to become a treasured heirloom appreciated by the next generation or two.

BIBLIOGRAPHY

Beatie, Russel H.
    1981 *Saddles.* Norman, OK:
          University of Oklahoma Press.
Dulaney, George
    1972 *Know All About Tack,* Title 117. Omaha, NE:
          Farnam Horse Library.
Edwards, E. Hartley
    1963 *Saddlery.* Cranbury, NJ:
          A.S. Barnes & Co.

Evans, Timothy H.
    1998 *The Sheridan Saddle and the Art of Don King.*
          Jackson, MS:
          University Press of Mississippi.
Gianoli, Luigi
    1967 *Horses and Horsemanship Through the Ages.* NY:
          Crown Publishers.
Grant, Bruce
    1951 *The Cowboy Encyclopedia.*
    1956 *How to Make Cowboy Horse Gear,*
          with a Section on How to Make a Western Saddle.
          Cambridge, MD: Cornell Maritime Press.
Hasluck, Paul Nooncree
    1962 *Saddlery and Harnessmaking.*
          London, UK: J.A. Allen & Co.

Hopper, John
    1982   *Cowboy's Complete Saddle Making.*
            Jackson Hole, WY: Chahala's Publishing Co.
Jeschko, Kurt and Harold Lange
    1972   *The Horse Today and Tomorrow.* London, UK:
            Kaye & Ward.
Jones, Dave
    1982   *Making and Repairing Western Saddles.* NY:
            Prentice Hall Press.
Johnson, Dusty
    1993   *Saddlemaking - Lessons in Construction, Repair and
            Evaluation* Loveland, CO:
            Saddleman Press.
Jones, William E.
    1972   *Anatomy of the Horse.* East Lansing, MI:
            Caballus Publishers.
Kahin., Dr. Sharon
    1993   *Saddlemaking in Wyoming.* Laramie, WY:
            University of Wyoming.
Laird, James R.
    1983   *The Cheyenne Saddle.* Cheyenne, WY:
            Frontier Printing, Inc.
Likewise, Bob
    1997   *Introductory Saddlemaking.* Great Falls, MT:
            Advanced Litho Printing.
Mora, Jo
    1946   *Trail Dust and Saddle Leather.* NY:
            Charles Scribner's Sons.
Myres, Sandra L.
    1961   *S.D. Myers: Saddlemaker.* Kerrville, TX.
            Privately printed.
Reed, Chuck
    1996   *Saddle Sense.* Rawlins, WY:
            Chuck Reed.

Rice, Lee M. and Glenn R. Vernam
    1975 *They Saddled the West.* Cambridge, MD:
           Cornell Maritime Press.
Settle, Mary Lund and Raymond W. Settle
    1955 *Saddles and Spurs.* NY:
           Crown Publishers.
Sherer, Richard L.
    1977 *Horseman's Handbook of Western Saddles.*
           Franktown, CO: Sherer Custom Saddles, Inc.
Steffen, Randy
    1967 *Horsemen Through Civiliazation.*
           Colorado Springs, CO:
           Western Horseman.
Stohlman, Al and Ann Stohlman
    1993 *The Stohlman Encyclopedia of Saddle Making.*
           Fort Worth ,TX: Tandy Leather Co.
Thomas, Carson
    1993 *The Western Saddle.* Hulett, WY:
           Jinglebob Publishing.
Tylden, G.
    1965 *Horses and Saddlery.* London, UK:
           J.A. Allen & Co.
Ward, Fay E.
    1958 *The Cowboy at Work.* NY:
           Hastings House.
Yates, Robin
    1976 *Western Saddle Making.*
    1984 *Advanced Western Saddle Making.* NSW, Australia:
           Robin Yates Western Saddlery.

PERIODICALS

Harness Shop News.
Monthly
347 Elk Road, Sylva, NC 28779.

Leather Crafters and Saddlers Journal.
Bimonthly
331 Annette Court, Rhinelander, WI 54501.

Old Cowboy Saddles and Spurs.
Annual
PO Box 529, Marion, IA 52302.

VIDEOS

Gomer, Bill
    1997   *Bill Gomer's Saddle Making.*
            Leavenworth, KS.:
            Bill Gomer/Moriah Productions

Johnson, Dusty
    1993   *Saddlemaking - Lessons in Construction, Repair*
          and Evaluation
            Loveland, CO:
            Saddleman Press.

Index

About the Illustrator

Doug Zender is the kind of illustrator that all authors pray to find. He listens, asks questions, thinks about the subject and draws with real interest and concern for accuracy.

Originally from Durango, Colorado, he was raised in both Colorado and California. After time in the U.S.Navy he did drawings in Spain for a short period before returning to his beloved Colorado. His specialties are visual appeal and effective layout for publications, logo design, large graphics and signs. Doug is also adept at brush lettering, calligraphy, airbrush art and vehicle graphics. He states that "letterform is a passion, not merely a vocation".

He currently lives in Loveland, Colorado, with his son Jeremy. He can be contacted at:

A to Z Unlimited
505 N. Cleveland Ave
Loveland, CO 80537

About theAuthor

Dusty Johnson began carving leather when he was about 12 years old. Growing up in Arizona and living in the high mountains of Colorado has given him the opportunity to spend time observing and learning from many of the recognized great leatherworkers of the West.

He has been a professional farrier for more than 20 years and has studied the interaction of the horse/rider/saddle at the many working ranches, guest ranches and livery stables where he has been employed.

After his formal education in Business Management at Northern Arizona University, Flagstaff, Dusty operated a jewelry manufacturing firm, worked as a marketing consultant for an advertising agency, was a licensed real estate broker, was on the staff of various equine and computer publications and was the managing editor of a midwestern newspaper.

The past 10 years have seen students from across the United States and many foreign countries learn to make and evaluate western saddles at his Loveland, Colorado, based Pleasant Valley Saddle Shop and School. The shop is named for an area where he spent time as a youth. The Pleasant Valley sits quietly in the shadow of the Mogollon Rim in central Arizona, also known as Young, Arizona.

He is the President of Pleasant Valley, Incorporated, and the author of books and videos of leatherworking instruction. He also writes for a variety of publications and presents leatherwork and marketing lectures nationwide.

Dusty and Sharon, his wife of 30+ years, live southwest of Loveland, Colorado, with an eclectic assortment of exotic vehicles, motorcycles, horses and a cat. They have two married daughters and (as of this writing) two grandchildren.

He can be contacted through:
        Saddleman Press, Box 909,Loveland, CO 80539

The Cowboy Craft Library
by
Dusty Johnson

SADDLEMAKING (Book, Video & Patterns)

The *Book* ($16.95) - Contains over 130 step-by-step photos and illustrations, accompanied by clear and concise text to lead the reader easily from raw materials to a handsome and useful finished saddle. No prior experience necessary.

The *Video* ($39.95) - An important companion to the book, it is nearly 2 hours of fast-paced, detailed instruciton showing EVERY step from start to finish.

The *Patterns* ($10.95) - Full size with cutting and skiving instructions. Any style or size saddle can be made by modifying these basic patterns.

CHAPS - Video & Patterns ($19.95)

Make your own riding chaps with this step-by-step instructional video. Every detail is shown clearly and explained fully. Each video is packaged with full-size patterns for Chinks, Batwings, Shotgun and Motorcycle chaps. No experience necessary. Use simple hand tools only. (35 min.)

HOLSTERS and Knife Sheaths -
Video & Patterns ($29.95)

Detailed instructions for making 5 different holsters, 3 knife sheaths and 2 gun belts. Full-size cutting and carving patterns included. No experience needed and use only simple hand tools. (65 min.)

Order Form

Please send the following books and videos:

	Price	Number	Total
Saddle Savvy (book)	$22.95		
Saddlemaking (book)	16.95		
Saddlemaking (video)	39.95		
Saddlemaking (patterns)	10.95		
Chaps (video & pattern)	19.95		
Holsters (video & pattern)	29.95		

Shipping: ($3 for the first item and $2 for each additional item

Total order

Name:_____

Address:_____

City:_____State:_____Zip:_____

Telephone: (_____)_____
Payment:
[ ] Cheque
[ ]VISA   [ ] MasterCard
Card Number:_____
Exp.Date:_____/_____
Signature_____

SADDLEMANPRESS™

PO Box 909, Loveland, Colorado, 80539
(800) 571-0021 FAX (970) 669-1589